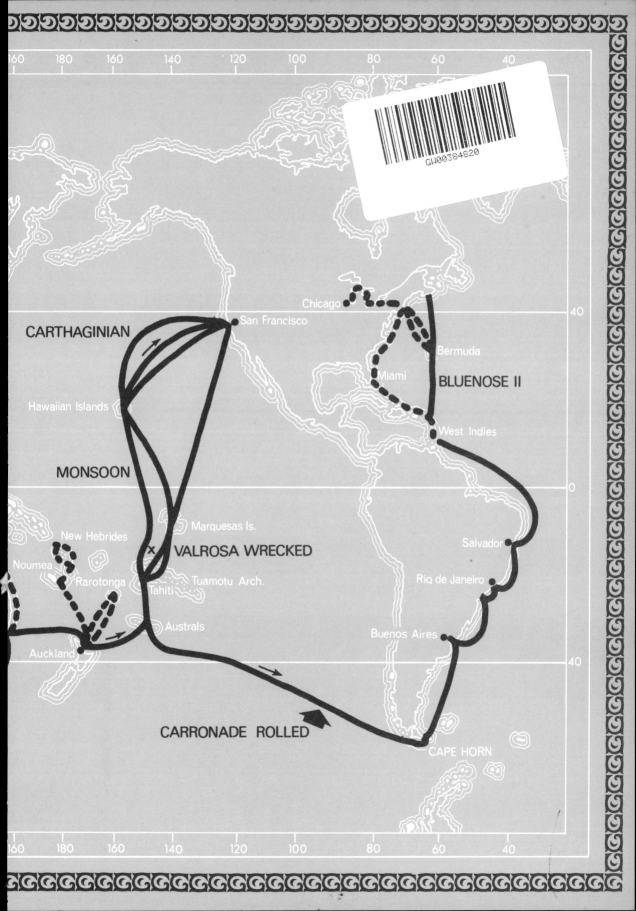

World Wanderer

WORLD WANDERER

100,000 miles under sail

Des Kearns

Carronade
Bluenose II
Valrosa
Monsoon
Carthaginian
Ondine

ANGUS AND ROBERTSON • PUBLISHERS

First published in 1971 by

ANGUS AND ROBERTSON (PUBLISHERS) PTY LTD
102 Glover Street, Cremorne, Sydney
2 Fisher Street, London
159 Boon Keng Road, Singapore
P.O. Box 1072, Makati MCC, Rizal, Philippines
107 Elizabeth Street, Melbourne
222 East Terrace, Adelaide
167 Queen Street, Brisbane

Reprinted 1973

National Library of Australia
card number and
ISBN 0 207 12263 6

©*Des Kearns 1971*

PRINTED IN HONG KONG

Episodes

To Andy Wall
and to Susie

Acknowledgements

In six years of voyaging round the world many people showed kindness and hospitality. I would particularly like to thank: "Flap" Martiningo, Alan Warwick, Docteur and Madame Huet, Madame Tetuanui Moana and the people of Tikehau Atoll, Hugh and Mimi Gordon, Tani Janes, Charles Borden, the people of Tierra del Fuego, Cesar Augusto Schang, the staff of the Buenos Aires Yacht Club, Bernard Bouts, Curt and Jenny Ashford, Helen Paine, Bobby Uriburu, and others.

Photographs

All photos are by Des Kearns except: "Sterling Hayden—sailor, writer and actor" by Hal Painter, *Rudder* Magazine; "*Bluenose II* under full sail" by Cal Productions, and "The original *Carronade* crew furling the main topsail" by Stan Bettis.

"Cleaning a good catch of bonito", "Sterling Hayden's former schooner, the magnificent *Wanderer*, wrecked on Rangiroa Atoll", "Paradise really exists —Rangiroa Atoll", and "Bob Nance on the track to Melville's famed Typee Valley" were photographed by Andrew Wall.

"Andy occupied on the *Carthaginian* in the ancient crafts of a sailor", "John Plummer and Des Kearns furling the main course", "Shakedown cruise through the Hawaiian Islands", "Mike Myers takes the *Carthaginian's* wheel", and "Each line has its set place" were photographed by Stan Bettis.

TYPE: Carmen-class sloop of oregon and spotted gum. COUNTRY: Australia. OWNER: Andrew Wall. YEAR OF CONSTRUCTION: 1964. BUILDER: Ron Swanson, Sydney. DESIGNERS: Wally Ward and Ron Swanson. DIMENSIONS: Overall length 30 feet; water-line length $24\frac{1}{2}$ feet; draught 5 feet; beam 9 feet 3 inches. DISPLACEMENT: 4.9 tons. BALLAST: $2\frac{1}{4}$ tons; 45% ballast ratio. SAILS: Dacron, Miller and Whitworth. RIG: 2 spinnakers, 2 mains (1 storm trysail), 4 headsails. HEIGHT OF MAST: 34 feet. ENGINE: 7 H.P. Volvo Penta diesel. FUEL CAPACITY: 5 gallons. CREW: 3. USE: World cruising.

ROUND THE CAPE
IN THE CARRONADE

From Sydney to the West Indies via Cape Horn in a 30-foot sloop

On the 26th March, 1967, just 500 miles from Cape Horn we were awed by what we saw and heard "beyond the common experience of men" . . .

Carronade was long past the point of no return and fast bringing up the latitude of the Cape. At the change of watch I remarked to Andy that the Southern Cross was directly overhead. Craning his neck to see it, he said quietly, "Yes, we're a long way south." The barometer had been falling for three days without change in weather. We had been lucky till then but now silently scanned the weather horizon waiting for the contest to begin. The barometer stood at 28.6, a quarter of an inch from the end of the scale; we shook with uncertainty and tenseness—waiting for the unknown, men fear most.

It all happened quickly; the steady increase in wind and sea, until by daybreak *Carronade* scudded before roaring seas under a gunmetal sky. We doused all sail and ran under bare poles. However, after driving uncontrollably down the faces of waves, at times reaching nine knots, we laid out a long warp of manilla rope, on the end of which was made fast a bight of chain and a motor scooter tyre to create extra drag—and still our speed increased so we laid out another and yet another warp, settling down to $6\frac{1}{2}$ knots with no sail and three warps. At one stage we surfed down the face of a huge sea, which later broke uninterrupted for 200 yards, the warps, chains and tyres leaping out of the water and ricocheting down the face.

We had been living roughly for the past ten days, eating our meals one at a time sitting on the cabin sole braced between the lower bunk and the saloon table. Because of the severe cold we needed to relieve ourselves at increasingly more frequent intervals. As the vessel was battoned down and wet on deck the only solution we found was to use a cocoa tin set aside for the purpose, open the tiny hatch an inch or two, and pour it into the cockpit (there was no "head" on board). For other needs we used a plastic bucket passing it out to the helmsman for disposal.

For heating devices we used a Tilley pressure lamp. However, having no flu, condensation soon formed on the deckhead and as time passed turned to green slime—everything became cold and greasy to the touch. Our sleeping bags were wet and we slept in wet clothes, but with wool next to the skin this presented no great problem.

We were not, strange as it may seem, miserable or uncomfortable, for we had conditioned ourselves to accepting all challenges. Our daily routine was so exacting and taxing we had no time to regret, complain, argue or even think about why we were there. In addition, there was a grand shared feeling that we were running our easting down as did the great clippers—nothing else mattered. None of us would fail, if this experience broadened perspectives, cultivated latent abilities and endowed us with confidence and courage. At all events—it was not our place to complain as we had chosen this way of life.

I was on the tiller when Andy opened the hatch with his bucket for the day. I reached cautiously for it and then yelled, "Hey! Andy, we're dead in the water!" We were in a giant trough, so deep that no wind penetrated, and the wave that rose up astern was almost vertical and unlike any he had ever seen— there was water cascading down like a waterfall. His face turned to horror as he blurted out "I've got to close this now." And apparently as he darted below he said to Bob, who was reading *Romeo and Juliet* in his bunk, "Say a quick prayer for Des." *Carronade,* after taking the brunt of the force, went down bow first, stood vertically on end for a moment before recovering and slewing sideways onto her beam ends and then rolled under the giant wave. How she was not dismasted will always be a mystery.

The next thing I knew there were tons of water toppling from the sky and a giant tearing noise seemed to wrench the boat apart. The only thing I remember is feeling crushed as the cockpit and finally the whole boat went over my head. From then on, I was under water in an upside down position; and we seemed to be sinking. The water temperature was 40° F. and yet I do not recall being cold. Suddenly *Carronade* righted herself shrugging off cascades of water. At the time of rolling I was lashed in by three life-lines, each with a breaking strain

8

Whale-gunner from Bequia, West Indies

Heaving-down an island schooner, St Barts

Primitive boat-building of inter-island schooners, Dominica

Careening in shallow water by Bequia shipwrights

Ushuaia in Argentina, southernmost town in the world

Sterling Hayden—sailor, writer and actor

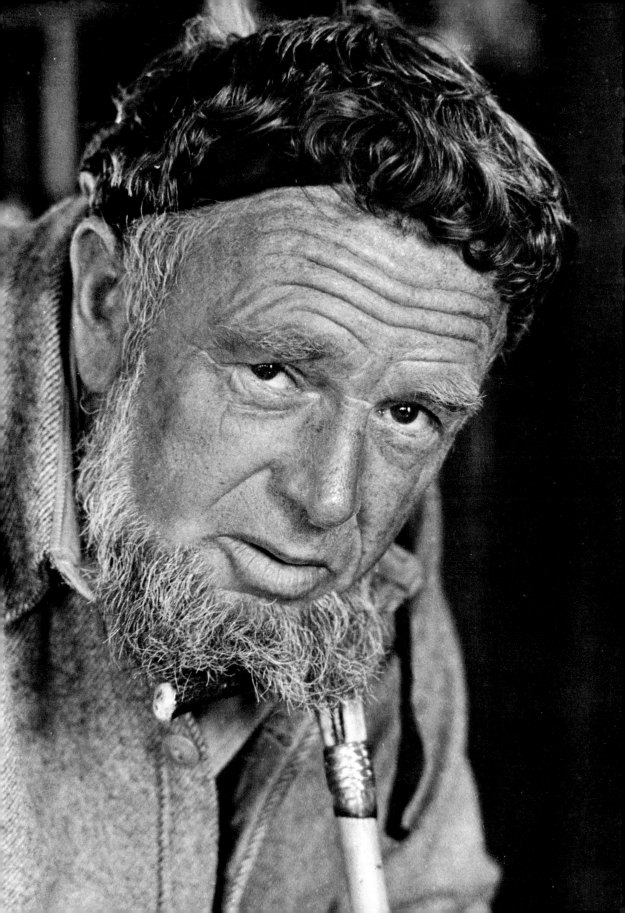

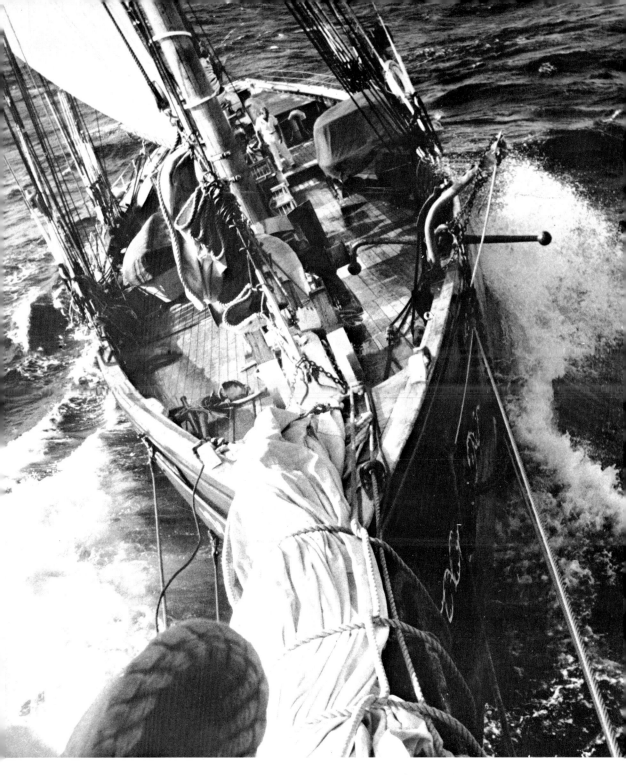

Bluenose II hove-to in a gale, North Atlantic

Bluenose II in warmer climes

Bluenose II under full sail

of one ton; and by a miracle one of the lines snagged on a winch pinning me in the steering position. I stood up bewildered and waist deep in icy water. *Carronade* seemed very low in the water and sluggish—I felt sure she was full but never considered the possibility of her going down. I don't remember being scared because in the past I had had similar experiences with surfboats capsizing, but in those days I could swim to the beach. Out here there was no land to swim to and even if there was, the maximum time a person can live in such cold water is 20 minutes—most perish within five.

In answer to a scream below, I said I was all right, or at least I thought I was; having so many clothes on and feeling numbed through I had no way of telling whether I was injured or not. I still felt the boat was full of water and though Andy and Bob said it was not serious I somehow didn't believe them, and as a reaction began furiously bailing the cockpit with the bucket, which miraculously was still in my hand—explaining the wrenched shoulder blade. No one ever flushed a toilet with that much water before, I thought.

The fibreglass spray dodger was completely smashed; the dinghy was broken in two; the lifebuoy broken in half (Lord knows how), but there was no apparent damage to the mast. In fact with the main hatch battened down the whole deck had been stripped and now resembled a canoe.

A terrifying loneliness seemed to grip me, and as I stood in the cockpit with tiller between my legs, the *Carronade* seemed smaller than before. There seemed to be no protection from the fury of the grey streaked walls of water occasionally colliding with one another and causing an avalanche of seething foam.

The amusing outcome of the incident was that when I asked Andy and Bob to come on deck to throw overboard the two halves of the dinghy, their immediate reaction was, not realizing the extent of the damage, "Christ! He's gone mad and wants to abandon ship."

All was bedlam below—food, bedding, charts and even the radios were soaked with sea-water. This was serious because without the radio we could no longer get time signals for navigation.

However, the worst was yet to come; as night fell, fierce hail and snow squalls swept over us. It seemed the Horn was battering us with all its fury. One could not even glance to windward without being blinded by driving sleet. The seas were getting bigger all the time, and we had more than 500 feet of line streamed astern to check the boat's speed. By midnight the gale was at its worst; the onrushing seas sounded like steam trains and the squalls were beyond human comprehension. We all agreed it was worse below, because we couldn't see what was going on. Imagination is always more frightening than what is seen.

The most any of us could take was an hour and a half on the helm. I vividly recall Andy and myself at the change of watch assuring each other that the barometer was beginning to rise. Andy would tap it with his finger; it would drop a fraction, "See that, it rose" I would say. "We're going to be all right". "Yes! Yes! It's going up" he would agree. I will never forget that night: a brilliant full moon blasted through the racing scud of clouds illuminating the breaking seas. Bob said that on the helm he had a feeling of superhuman power.

9

As he encountered each onrushing wall of water he felt he was controlling the sea at its mightiest. Andy said *Carronade* seemed to know what was expected of her and rose gallantly to the biggest of seas. This was the experience of our lives... Yes, we were scared, but here in the Southern Ocean, Nature has a proving ground in which she can demonstrate what she can do. How many times in one's lifetime does one ever get the opportunity to see Nature at her finest? In this dimension, when the sea is roughest, it is also most beautiful.

The grand finale came when a squall struck with such violence and intensity that it turned the entire sea white. The shrieking of that squall will always live with me. I kept saying to myself "Steer you bastard steer. If one of these brute crests catches us beam on, we'll all go to the bottom." When the squall abated, all suddenly calmed. It seemed to be the last defiant blast from nature telling us she had let us through.

It seems incredible that by midday we had a spinnaker set and under clear sunny skies we romped towards the Horn. At the time of rolling we were baking bread in our kerosene oven. However, after the incident, the oven was nowhere to be found. Bob discovered it up forward in the sail locker, the half-baked bread still intact. After rebaking, it turned out to be one of the best loaves of the passage. Spirits were high and Andy composed a rhyme:

> And when I reach the Pearly Gates,
> To Saint Peter I can tell . . .
> One more Cape Horner reporting Sir,
> For I've served my time in Hell!

•   •   •   •

The circumstances that led to my being caught in a gale off Cape Horn had their roots two years earlier. I was now twenty years old and had left home about two years ago, rejecting a career as a trainee executive in the pursuit of freedom and adventure by way of the sea. I learned the rudiments of small-boat sailing off the Queensland coast and from there I progressed to New Zealand and an old South Seas trading schooner, the *Tiare Taporo,* on which I sailed for nine months among the Cook Islands and those of the New Hebrides and New Caledonia.

I subsequently returned to Sydney and met up with an old friend, Ken Mills, who informed me of his intentions to sail round the world in a thirty-foot sloop belonging to another young Australian, Andy Wall. Some weeks later I happened to meet Andy at a party and before I knew what I had done I found myself included in these preparations. We set ourselves a deadline departure date and worked feverishly day after day to meet it, finally being waved away from Andy's little wharf at Avalon in Sydney on 21st March, 1965, by a small band of somewhat sceptical wellwishers. I might add that by the time we reached Barrenjoey we were all thoroughly sick and there ensued a most uncomfortable passage across the Tasman to New Zealand on which we set a new passage record of 7 days and 3 hours, much to our amazement and disbelief, as we had been too ill to move out of our bunks for much of the time.

10

Two years separated this initial passage of the *Carronade* from our final leavetaking for the Horn in San Francisco. I wandered through the fabled South Seas on *Carronade* for several months and then left her in Tahiti in order to improve on my now non-existent finances by working on a variety of larger boats. When I eventually rejoined *Carronade* in San Francisco, I found that Ken had returned to Australia to marry and his place had been taken by another Aussie, Bob Nance. It must have been in the back of Bob's mind for many years to sail round the Horn—ever since his brother Bill had made a single-handed rounding in 1963—but it was not until the age of 26 that he finally walked out of a career in banking. Andy Wall on the other hand, had started this venture at the age of 22 when he gave up a career in accountancy and had *Carronade's* hull professionally built. He chose an Australian-designed Carmen Class sloop that had proved its worth repeatedly as an efficient and fast boat, and from an empty shell fitted her out himself with great foresight and practical common sense.

Two years had passed—with adventures and misadventures—before we at last came together on the *Carronade* to get ready to sail, via the Pacific Islands, for the Cape.

•　　　•　　　•　　　•

We had become part of the community in San Francisco and it was hard to leave. The previous Sunday there had been a special church service to wish us well. In the early morning fog we ghosted down the bay, and the deep-throated growl of Alcatraz bid us farewell. On the bridge above, barely visible commuters passed on their way to the office. Foghorns seemed to be everywhere, distant strident tones all mixed and lost in the thick damp wool of the fog. Feeling insignificant and lonely we rounded the San Francisco lightship and laid the course for the 3300-mile passage to Nuku Hiva in the Marquesas Islands which *Carronade* would make in the remarkable time of 24 days. *Carronade* never ceased to amaze us with her ability to maintain good daily mileage in light or heavy conditions.

From our Sailing Ship Directory, dated 1898, we read that: ". . . Captains are advised not to put into the Marquesas Islands lest they should lose half their crew to the licentious women."

These were the Marquesas, the desolate isles, the wilderness isles, the islands that always were outcasts, but never more so than now. Far more than Oceania, this land had known the wrath of the white man, for the Marquesan has resented being enslaved. He fought back when they chained him and shipped him to the hellish guano islands off Peru. He fought back when the pious Yankee whaleships came in quest of brawny harpooners and moist warm island girls. And he fought back when the traders swindled him out of his land and the missions laid siege on his soul.

In less than 100 years the Marquesans were all but extinguished. In 1800, the population was estimated at 85,000. A century later because of disease, debauch, suppression, and outright slaughter, the pitiful remnant numbered less than 2600 among the dozen islands that comprize the archipelago.

It was hot and quiet as we drifted down the bay, ghosted along by catspaws of wind. The village of Tiaohae (population 200—the largest village in the group), nestled hard up against the deeply-weathered precipitous cliffs. The unusual, awesome peaks and green lush slopes dropped almost sheer to black sand beaches—peaceful, protected and steaming with humidity. The concave shoreline was broken by a small peninsula, on top of which stood a range-light for ships approaching at night.

The passage to Nuku Hiva was over—we were in the islands. No longer did *Carronade* pitch and toss; as day gave way to night, we were tired but at peace with the world—San Francisco seemed far away.

•　　　•　　　•　　　•

At a neat yellow and brown cottage with a verandah overlooking the bay in Nuku Hiva, we met a real character, Dick Sixberry—and his Tahitian wife, Moea. Dick was a shell collector for the Smithsonian Institute in Washington. He told us many yarns of the islands. He smoked "Bison" roll-your-own cigarettes and had a habit of smoothing away his airforce-type moustache so it would not get in his mouth. He was no more than 35, yet looked 50—heavy drinking, obesity and signs of baldness made him look much older. Nevertheless, I have never met a more agreeable fellow. He did most of his diving at night, which sounded a pretty dangerous occupation to me. We drank Hinano beer with him and ate from cans of Communist Chinese food containing small greaseproof packages of duck, tripe, fish and chicken.

On another verandah we chatted with veteran trader Bob McKitrick, now 87. His arms were tatooed sailor-fashion with hearts, anchors and clasped hands. Despite his years in the islands, he had not lost his Liverpool brogue. His seafaring days were long in the past, but he had not lost his consuming love of the sea. He had thrashed round the Horn in big square-riggers, watched knife fights in the streets of lawless ports on the Chilean coast, and had been blown ashore when a typhoon swept up the Hoogly River. Trader Bob was a relic of the past when a seaman's life was cheap and the mates used brass knuckles to keep the crew at work. Bob's mind tended to wander, he was almost blind and he had the shakes in his left hand. He called us sundowners and kept asking us whether the big German four masters were still running out to Sydney and Melbourne.

•　　　•　　　•　　　•

After the high volcanic islands of the Marquesas, we set a course for the Tuamotu Archipelago. There is nothing as enchanting as a landfall on a Tuamotuan atoll. Palm trees rise from the sea like a mirage. As we came closer, the palms seemed to be joined to the horizon by a thin strip of golden sand. Two hundred yards from the roar of the surf, we scudded along the edge of the reef and set our big spinnaker. The small sleek sloop, the deep blue sea and the atoll, white-tipped with sand and spume, were set against a backdrop of green coconut palms and a steel-grey sky. We could see the turquoise hues of the inner lagoon, then the break in the reef, through which we ran *Carronade,* rounding up to bring her alongside under sail. Several Tahitians leapt aboard to help make fast and clean up the decks. Suddenly there was a hand on my shoulder and an old shipmate, Tapu, whom I had met while sailing in the Pacific, welcomed me to Manihi.

I looked up at my favourite atoll. It hadn't changed a bit since the day I celebrated my 21st birthday here, two years ago. The long wharf stretched before us, bleached white and spotlessly clean. On the end near the lagoon, stood a battered whitewashed building used for storing pearl shell. In the centre of the wharf, a huge Tou tree provides the only real shelter and a place for spontaneous sing-songs as the sun goes down. Towards the seaward side lies one of the wonders of the South Seas—a shark pool, some 60 feet long and 2 feet deep. *Rairi* is the native name for the sharks—the longest being about 7 feet, the smallest 5 feet. They are completely harmless and young Polynesian children have a wonderful time being towed round the pool, hanging onto the sharks' tails or dorsal fins. A whitewashed monument, flagstaff and French Ensign stand at the end of the pool, and in the village the red steeple of the Catholic church towers above all. Thick coral cement walls line the picturesque streets (if you could call them streets). Once these walls were a sign of status—now they are only used to keep pigs out. In a doorway a mother can be seen breastfeeding a child, while in another a copious, pareu-clad grandmother shooes away dogs and picks up a child to shower it with affection.

Tapu beckoned us to his house for a bath, and explained that his wife was already killing a pig and a dog for a feast in our honour. The pork was delicious and I suppose the dog was quite tasty except for the fact that uppermost in our minds was the thought that it was dog. Tapu's wife's father had died at the age of 71 on the neighbouring atoll of Ahe and we were asked to be his guest at the funeral the next day.

The following morning we set out in a 20-foot open boat, which I thought was unsuitable for the open sea. Tapu explained that he sometimes visits atolls 60 or 80 miles away and never uses a compass. Pointing out to sea, he said "We just know where to go." The whole village turned out to see us off. We were accompanied by the owner of the boat, the owners of the two outboard engines, various relatives, four cans of gas, some mangos, bread and water. Away we went, hoisting a small sail made from flour bags to act as a steadying sail—and our only hope of salvation if the outboards gave out.

The pass at Ahe was wide, with dangerous surf flanking each side. Inside the lagoon, an arm of coral formed the protective anchorage along the island itself. The funeral began mid-afternoon. In a small *fare-nihau* (palm-thatch hut) each close relative kissed the dead man in his coffin; the lid was fitted and then the coffin carried by bearers to the graveyard. No one looked very sad, and I tried not to laugh when I noticed some of the graves were marked out by empty beer bottles. In typical Polynesian style they discovered the grave was too short for the box, so someone shovelled out some more sand. One of the bearers got his leg caught between the coffin and the grave, and finally fell in, to everyone's delight. The box was settled, but at a serious moment someone laid a boot into a troublesome dog, again disrupting the ceremony. Then each of us threw our Tiare Tahiti flowers on top of the coffin, the grave was covered, and the most moving and heart-warming spiritual singing followed. That evening, so the widow would not be sad, she had to lead the singing at the feast, which was held in her honour.

As *Carronade* drew away from Manihi, Tapu waved for a long time. Another friend left behind, I thought. Soon the atoll was gone and we rolled for Tahiti, where we would do our final fitting out for the southward journey to Cape Horn.

In Tahiti refitting took us six weeks and was completed without undue fuss; one morning in late February we quietly let go the mooring lines and slipped out of Papeete harbour for the last time. We said nothing about our destination because at that time Chichester's voyage was much publicized and we were afraid of being branded young fools following in his wake.

Cape Horn is nothing more than an island at the coccyx of the great Andean spine. Resembling a clenched fist, it stands like a sentinel between two great oceans—and is the last word in the lexicon of sailormen: its ironbound reputation has put fear into men's hearts for centuries.

The ships that discovered Cape Horn were commanded by Cornelius Schouten, whose expedition was financed by the merchants of Hoorn in Holland, and principally by one—Le Maire Schouten. They passed between Staten and the mainland, Le Maire's son naming the strait after his father. They beat past Cape Horn in 1615, and he generously and modestly christened the "Horn" after his home town. The ship in which he sailed also had the same name—*Hoorn*.

Today there are an increasing number of small-boat sailors making the hazardous passage, each adding a little knowledge about this relatively untouched corner of the globe. The Argentinian Vito Dumas once wrote: "Lives there a sailor who would not have made a Cape Horn passage in his own small vessel rather than any other voyage in the world?" Cape Horn took on a new light, a new meaning, when we knew we were going down there to actually experience all the fears and adventures we had read about.

Our course took us south through trade winds and calms to the more boisterous and feared Roaring Forties belt where we ran down our easting in the wake of the old Cape Horn clippers. And it was in an area 500 miles from the Horn that we experienced our ultimate storm and the rolling of our little sloop.

●　　　●　　　●　　　●

On Thursday 30th March, 1967, four days after our wild storm experience, Andy did a splendid job of navigation, obtaining the usual sun sights, a sight of the moon and several evening star sights, and from these laid a course that enabled us to pass between Ildefonso and Diego Ramirez islands—a tense night as we saw neither. During the long and lonely hours of my watch I remembered old Captain Boulton's words . . . "beware of the islands of Diego Ramirez, they stick out of the sea like ugly black teeth."

At 5 a.m. Andy sighted land. The day opened grey, the sea was calm, and we were in the lee of the land. Land was starting to appear everywhere. The sun rose red beneath a low grey sky. Then we saw no more of it. The coast became clear and we could see the Darwin Ranges, silver blue and snow-covered. Both the land and the sea appeared grey and white-capped. Then we picked up False Cape Horn, Hermite Island and finally Horn Island, standing out alone. To the south lay the unknown; it was difficult to distinguish the horizon. Antarctica lay some 600 miles into that silver wilderness.

Andy braced himself against the mast, chart in hand identifying each point of land or island; Bob and I were both in the cockpit. Very few words were spoken as each of us lost himself in thought as to what this landfall meant personally. I believe that we all felt a sense of achievement. For the first time in our lives we had done something of which we could feel proud. It did not matter what the rest of the world thought, the important thing became the personal sense of a goal attained.

During the night of the gale we had cut our watches down to one and a half hours because that was as much as any man could stand. Scared out of my wits, just before emerging on deck I told the others I wouldn't last more than half an hour; but somehow if I was ever going to live with myself again I had to do it. I knew their lives were in my hands and something told me to go out there and fight and fight.

After the big gale we drove *Carronade* on towards the Horn before we took another beating. The work was hard and the sail changes many. We cursed, moaned and groaned and had trivial arguments, but there was great team spirit —we worked as one man towards our goal. To this day one of my clearest memories of Bob is his fixed gaze on that blue-grey morning when, without looking at me and in a barely audible voice, he said "It's like nothing I've ever seen; it has a cold stark beauty." Bob was not one to openly display feeling or sentiment but in his own quiet way he put more feeling into this than anything I had ever heard him say before.

Ten miles from the Cape we could see our anchorage for the night, Port Maxwell. The sea had changed colour to a murky green-grey, the sun was reflected off the snow-covered peaks of the Darwin Ranges, and Cape Horn took on colour and substance. The wind freshened a little and *Carronade* gulped up the last of the long sea miles to close the distance between us and our dream. The salt spray stung our faces but we all stayed on deck to savour these moments. As we drew near the great granite bastion, we thought of all the clipper ships that had thumped their way through these same Drake Straits—over-canvassed, with flooded fo'c's'les and heart-breaking work on dizzy yards, of their ill-clad men driven by masters blind to suffering and exhaustion. Today the albatross and the other numerous sea birds must be lonely without the passing clouds of white canvas.

Everything was in accord for the great moment—the sea, the spectacular coast, the grey scudding sky, the weather-beaten vessel, and the haggard but high-spirited crew. We passed abeam at 11.50 a.m. The cliffs, when we drew near were sheer, black and jagged. We then threw over the side a shoe horn, bearing the inscription, "Practise going around this first", that had been presented to us by friends in San Francisco.

Once past the promontory we found the eastern side more hospitable with green slopes and a bay that would be suitable for landing on calm days. The wind fell and it was obvious that we could not make Port Maxwell with a safe margin of time; so consulting the chart, we decided to sail east of Herschel Island and anchor in what the Pilot Book called "a safe anchorage free from williwaws". We passed numerous patches of thick kelp and some dangerous sea-washed rocks and slowly progressed up the channel. Meanwhile, the barometer had dropped to 29.15 inches and from this steady downward progress we knew it would soon begin to blow. Several times we came within a few yards of Deceit Island—a spectacular bare shale and granite outcrop.

In the approaches of our anchorage, Puerto Piedrabuena, a rain squall passed over, bringing gale force winds. We doused Genoa and set storm jib. Several snow-capped peaks about us took on interesting colours and though only 3 p.m., at this time the scene resembled a late evening sunset on a stormy day. The wind blew strongly, and we made tack after tack. To our surprise there was a house with a high radio aerial on a headland north of our anchorage. Probably a sheep farmer or weather station we thought. There were a few anxious moments as we fought for the last mile—the last of 5,000—until finally within a few yards of the kelp and deep in the bay we dropped both anchors.

This was late afternoon. As Bob prepared the evening meal we heard the crack of a rifle. I took the glasses but could see no one ashore. Bob saw him first: a lone man upon the wind-blown slopes, dressed in grey and waving a white rag to attract our attention. He obviously wanted us to come ashore; however, night was approaching and the wind was strong. Though he was some distance from us, we managed to converse by signs quite easily. We held up our oars and criss-crossed our arms to denote that we had no dinghy, and held up the Australian flag as recognition. He waved vigorously as if he understood, took his white rag, wrapped it round his neck, lifted his rifle over his shoulder, and walked slowly and forlornly among the bare trees bent from the wind, and then disappeared over the hill. We estimated he had a long walk ahead of him if he was the inhabitant of the dwelling on the headland.

This hit us deeply. We had travelled 5,000 miles to the most fascinating corner of the world and could not go ashore because we had lost our dinghy in a gale en route to Cape Horn. Who was this lone soul? He would dearly love to seek our company and we his, but this was not possible. I shall always connect Cape Horn with this apparition on the hillside.

The following day we decided to get ashore no matter what happened. We

16

The Australian sloop Carronade at anchor in Bora Bora

Slaughtering our lamb, a gift from a Chilean farmer
Carronade and the American cutter Tehani share the hurricane hole at Bora Bora

Battened and prepared for Cape Horn weather
Cape Horn abeam—30th March, 1967

Tierra del Fuego—looking south towards the Beagle Canal
Fjord-like bay with the "Teeth of Navarino" in the background

Sugar Loaf Mountain, sentinel of Rio Harbour
Carronade rail-down in a smother of foam

Collecting earthy water in the remotest corner of the world
Our first time ashore on bleak Herschel Island, five miles from Cape Horn

Andy Wall waiting for the sun to reach its zenith
Baking bread in the tropics was not an unpleasant task

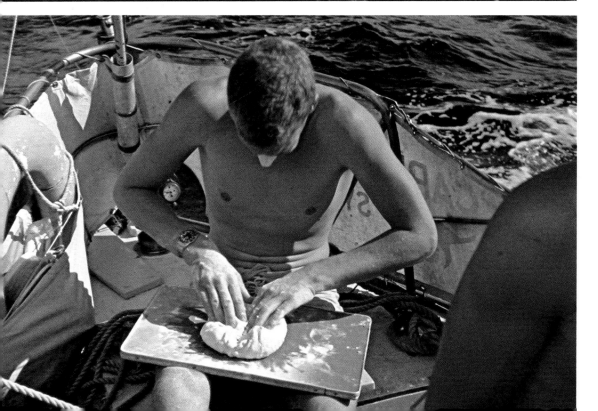

Carronade becalmed 600 miles south of Tahiti

thought of building an outrigger raft with our plastic water tanks, but in these windy conditions we could never row a clumsy raft. So we inflated our emergency life-raft, removed the awning and provisions, waited for a lull in the wind, and pulled for the shore.

The first step ashore was quite a momentous one. We stood at the foot of a soggy cliff on an island five miles from Cape Horn. *Carronade* was anchored out in the middle of the bay. We bent every spare piece of line together to make a life-line between her stern and the shore—buoying the line with yellow floats to prevent it from sagging in the thick kelp near the shore. If a sudden squall came up, we would be able to get back to *Carronade*. Looking like Polar explorers we struck out for the house seen on the barren headland a day earlier.

In a region such as this one cannot take enough precautions. When Cook visited this area he recorded that two of his men were caught out at night and consequently perished from the cold. No one knew we were here and no facilities were available for a rescue party. We carried packs containing waterproof matches, oilskins, dried fruit and a flashlight. Our legs were wobbly as this was the first time on solid ground in six weeks. The temperature was cold but after climbing the soggy cliff we began to sweat freely inside our heavy clothing. Then followed a long march over harsh ground. There were no paths, so we picked our way as best we could through the hardy scrub, sometimes over our heads. The ground underfoot resembled English peat and was like walking on a huge sponge. With the high rainfall, vegetation quickly rots and becomes mulch and new vegetation replaces the old.

A picture that sticks vividly in my mind is the approach to the cabin. I had fallen behind about 200 yards and stopped to catch my breath. Andy's and Bob's yellow oilskins contrasted sharply with the deep green of the rolling hills, and in the distance stood the desolate rust-coloured house, with the gloomy bare rock of Freycinet Island rising majestically towards the clouds.

Two young Chilean fellows came to meet us and escorted us inside. The house was stoutly constructed of timber and corrugated iron, with three chimneys and a high radio antenna. Carcasses of freshly killed meat hung outside the back door. It was surprisingly spartan inside—bare wooden floor, central wood-burning stove, table and chairs and a tall locker in one corner covered with nude pictures faded with age. The remaining room contained two bunks, a mass of radio equipment and a rack of high-powered rifles. Two sheepskin coats hung by the door and on the wall facing the bunks was a detailed chart of the surrounding islands.

Señors Eliecer Rodriguez and Rodolfo Gardenas of the Chilean Navy introduced themselves to us. We learnt each other's named by writing them on a piece of paper and repeating them slowly. With the use of a dictionary (that we had brought with us), and sign language they told us they manned this station for the Chilean Navy as a look-out for enemy shipping—the Argentinians; they and Chileans are continually having disagreements over territorial rights. Occasionally shots were exchanged.

It was a grand afternoon. We ate mutton, hot Chile sauce and homemade bread, washing it all down with a local Chilean firewater called Aguardiente. It was warm, snug and friendly inside while through the thick glass window we could see a gale blowing and snow falling. Two groups of men from opposite sides of the world, neither speaking the other's language and yet each revelling in the other's company and having a good time in this remotest of posts.

It was late in the afternoon so we bade our new-found friends farewell and promised to return on the morrow. As we left they began sending out Morse Code to Puerto Williams, who in turn would inform Valparaiso, and perhaps even our families. On returning to the dinghy we had overlooked the tide—a serious mistake—the rock to which the line was made fast was underwater and we had to risk rowing to the first buoy to recover the towline. On board, our snug little home was a veritable haven, protected from the elements outside and warmed down below by our Tilly pressure lamp.

In general, the area is a labyrinth of channels and islands and seems to be useless to man because of the harsh terrain and climate. Where the shores are not bare rock, they are covered with scrubby evergreen forest, which, at 1,000 feet peters out into boggy moor, rock and ice. This bleak landscape is swept summer and winter by high winds and persistent rain. Sudden changeability of weather is probably the most noticeable feature of the area; and later, we discovered this the hard way.

Wind howled in the rigging all night and squalls of great intensity passed over. The next day, 1st April, we struck out for the shore to replenish our freshwater supply and say farewell to the Chileans. The fresh water, however, was a dirty brown colour and tasted quite earthy. We found a small mountain stream that trickled down onto the beach and this seemed cleaner than most. Once again we stumbled over the boggy moor, and were caught without cover in a squall, lashed by sleet, and wet through. We had long ceased to worry about small discomforts, as this was a hard land for hard people and we had no choice but to adjust. We had to condition ourselves to think before each action; it was a land with no room for mistakes.

We made the Chileans a present of some canned mushrooms, canned bacon and a dozen eggs. On saying farewell they gave us a bottle of Aguardiente "to guard against the cold". Good for stoking a belly fire they gestured. Their spell of duty lasts five months, and we were the only people they had seen in the first three.

Snow fell overnight, with a small amount of ice on deck when we arose. With the anchor hove short we noticed one of the Chileans running down the hillside, yelling and waving. We couldn't understand so we waved goodbye and set out towards our next anchorage. The weather looked fine, with a light westerly breeze, but as we sailed past the cabin on the headland the other naval man was shouting and indicating to go back. "These bloody Spaniards really get excited don't they?" remarked Andy. The weather looked good so we proceeded north and entered the Franklin Canal. Without warning the sky turned blue-black, and the darkest squall we had ever seen enveloped everything as it approached. The canal was only half a mile wide, with jagged cliffs on either side. Taking a

18

quick compass bearing down the channel before the squall struck, we turned and under trysail alone ran blindly through the snow hoping our bearing had been correct. The squall passed and *Carronade's* sails, mast and deck were encased in ice. For times such as this, before leaving we had planned several alternative anchorages. We ran all the way back to a small bay north of our last anchorage, though it proved to be not as sheltered. The wind was still strong so we drove *Carronade* headlong into the thick matted kelp before letting go both anchors. This provided ideal protection.

After a quick meal we again ferried our craft and life-line ashore in between snow and hail squalls. Back in the welcome warmth of the cabin, we enjoyed our second midday meal of mutton soup, spaghetti bolognaise and home-made bread with a few tots of Aguardiente, which brought on a healthy glow. Our friends explained that the Chilean Navy had refused permission for us to use the Franklin and Murray canals as an access to the Beagle Canal. They claimed this was a safety measure against the strong currents and dangerous williwaws. However, we realized their motives were political, for our intended route would lead us to an Argentinian port, whereas their recommended route would lead us to a Chilean port. We had no choice but to enter the Beagle Canal from the east. Our next anchorage would be uninhabited, inhospitable Wollaston Island, 20 miles to the north.

Anchor watches were necessary throughout the night. Twice we had to shift anchors as the wind had changed, leaving us exposed to some swell; and with the falling tide we began hitting bottom. A safe anchorage was eventually found a few yards from shore behind a kelp bed that acted as a breakwater. It was an anxious night and in some ways we were glad to see the last of the Wollaston and Hermite Group. By midday the weather was clear and we left for Caleta Middle on Wollaston. With clear skies and calm seas, we experienced some fine sailing, enhanced by the solitude and beauty of the area—granite peaks, purple cliffs and distant snow-covered mountains all slowly changing colour in the sunset.

Suddenly a boat moving at high speed approached us and roared alongside. It was a camouflaged Chilean gunboat equipped with torpedoes and heavy armament on deck, and powered by two huge diesel engines, with a top speed of 45 knots. Quickly we ran up our flag. The bearded crew resembling polar men lined the rails and speculated among themselves, while the Captain addressed us in English.

We must have looked quite a sight: a small sloop, now resembling a canoe with its stripped deck and smashed doghouse, manned by three young men. "Do you know you are in Chilean waters? Have you charts? Have you food?" he asked in quick succession. We told him everything was all right. We were the sloop *Carronade*, two years out of Australia, last port of call Papeete, Tahiti, bound for Puerto Williams in the Beagle Canal. It so happened they were from Puerto Williams, and had come to welcome us and tow us to their base. We inquired what their slowest towing speed was and were told that it was fifteen knots with both engines idling and ten knots with one engine. As *Carronade's* maximum towing speed was only seven knots, we thanked them, pointed to Caleta Middle and arranged to rendezvous in the approaches of Puerto Williams. As they roared away we thought of all the biscuits and ice cream on board, for we longed for something sweet. Andy also remarked "I was half tempted to ask for a pack of cigarettes."

The following day we entered the Beagle Canal and experienced exhilarating sailing in a region that we believe must resemble the fjords of Norway. There was a direct contrast between the islands round the Horn and the colourful canal. By day we crept insignificantly up the waterway, dwarfed by the cypress and pine forests, flanking the water's edge with autumn tints of red, brown, yellow and purple. At night we anchored in snug harbours beside the silent, unforgettable mountains with snow swirling off their peaks.

We stopped at Puerto Eugenia, a land-locked anchorage and sheep station. A small verandahed farmhouse with the aroma of wood smoke drifting from its stone chimney, nestled against the brow of a hill. It was early morning, a boat put out from shore, and in the quiet of the fjord we could hear the gentle lapping of the paddles. A Chilean gentleman dressed in a well-cut tweed coat addressed us in perfect English. "I bring you fresh meat" he said and presented us with a lamb. At first we tethered the animal to the mast, but since that wouldn't be satisfactory when sailing, we lashed it to the stern pulpit until our arrival in Puerto Williams.

A committee of naval craft welcomed us to Puerto Williams. The commander of the base stepped on board *Carronade* and ordered a vessel to take us in tow. Once alongside, young naval officers sprang aboard and began clearing away the decks and furling the sails for us. We were bearded and hadn't had a bath for six weeks. They instructed us that *Carronade* would be taken care of and we could have quarters ashore to bath, clean up and take our meals. Andy and I jumped at the chance but Bob claimed he had slept in the same bunk for the past two years and preferred it to any ashore. Haircuts, shaves, hot showers and clean clothes—what a wonderful thought. I am quite sure they did not recognize us as the same fellows who had sailed in a few hours earlier. I in particular must have looked dreadful as shortly after leaving Tahiti, I shaved off my hair; and now hair and beard were the same length. We also took our sheep ashore, tethering him to a post in a lush grazing area where he could fatten himself up —for tomorrow we hoped to have lamb chops for dinner.

The Chileans greatly respect sail, for they spend part of their training on the barquentine *Esmeralda* and frequently visit Sydney, our home port. In true naval tradition we arrived on the dot of eight to meet a gathering of the English-speaking officers—the doctor, the gunboat captain, his navigator, and the commander and his attractive wife. We drank cognac and orange, and it wasn't long before the conversation flowed freely in English and Spanish, with French as a go-between when stuck for a word. The gunboat captain, an impressive fellow, spoke English well and had an exceptional knowledge of Chilean waters. Captain Camus told us that even he had to run for cover in the Franklin Canal while on his way south to stand-by in case Chichester needed assistance. The young navigator was a suave, immaculately dressed officer, who by his actions could never make a social error. If someone needed a match, he would stand up stiffly and, using only his index finger and thumb, unfasten the second brass button of his jacket, reach in with a Napoleon-like action and produce an expensive cigarette lighter, which ignited with a flick of the thumb. When the cognac was gone there appeared a bottle of Pisco (a favourite Chilean drink) to finish off the night—but in fact it finished off the commander, who lay prostrate in his chair incapable of intelligible speech. He did however promise to telegram our families and offered us free anything we may need. At midnight we adjourned to our heated officer's-quarters and clean beds.

The following day was a work day. Carrying buckets of scalding water from the boiler room in the timber mill near by, we washed our filthy clothes in a rather crude fashion on the wharf. With more scalding water we scoured down below in *Carronade*. But when it came to killing the sheep there were no volunteers. We all drooled at the thought of lamb chops but none of us quite knew how to go about it. Bob had seen a pig killed, and suggested it must be a similar operation. We drew straws for who would cut his throat and I lost. Andy brought the poor lamb down with a rugby tackle, I drove the knife in and finally "Skinner Bob" took over. Meanwhile the doctor, the dentist and the engineer arrived on the scene. The dentist informed me that a trick worth knowing is to slit one of the sheep's ankles after it has been killed, insert a connecting piece of a bicycle pump and simply blow him up. Apparently the skin is easily separated from the inner layers in this way. After cutting up the carcase we hung the meat in the rigging, and the temperature was sufficiently low to keep it fresh for some time.

The following day I recorded in my log: Due to hard work and severe cold our enormous hunger continues. Our intake of food would shock the normal eater. For breakfast we each consumed a bowl of porridge, two eggs, six lamb chops, toast, jam and coffee. Our evening meal consisted of what looked to me like half a sheep, but which we referred to as "leg of lamb".

One morning the dentist visited *Carronade* and, noticing our smashed fibreglass spray dodger, offered his services. At first we did not take him seriously when he told us to bring the doghouse to the naval hospital the following morning. However we did, carrying the shattered pieces on our shoulders, and were led to the operating theatre by the naval doctor. The cabin was laid on the operating table like a sick patient. The dentist, using his tooth drill, cut grooves across the cracks or tears, and inserted reinforcing pieces of stainless steel wire, bonding all together with the pink acrylic resin normally used for making denture plates. The finished job was excellent but in the process fibreglass particles scattered all over the operating theatre. Surely we thought, this must be the first time in history that a dentist had used denture material to repair a ship's cabin on a hospital operating table.

It is amusing to note that national prestige is the sole reason for the existence of Puerto Williams. Before the birth of Puerto Williams, the Argentinian town Ushuaia was the southernmost town in the world. It is all part of the petty jealous war that is continually waged between Chile and Argentina. Puerto Williams has a population of a mere 250 and consists only of a few shacks, a timber mill, and a small pier. But it has a tremendous collection of warships—six gunboats, a cruiser and supply vessel. The two countries even went as far as to divide the water in the Beagle Canal. Chile claimed Cape Horn as its territory and constructed a small lighthouse at the base of one of the fierce cliffs. The Argentinians sent down a gunboat and blasted it off the face of the cliff, but another was soon erected. Little wonder that Chichester, when asked how he found Cape Horn, replied "Crowded", after being informed that gunboats from the Chilean and Argentinian navies would be standing by in case he needed assistance.

Ushuaia has a population of about 3,000. Founded by the missionary, Thomas Bridges, as a haven for shipwrecked sailors it soon became a small town. And today its inhabitants are all descendants of sealers, whalers, sheep farmers, gold prospectors, retired sea captains and shipwrecked mariners who never returned to their homelands. All nationalities can be found there. It is a town of corrugated iron houses and muddy streets with many monuments. It nestles hard up against the soaring peaks of the Darwin Ranges. One is awed by the delicate blue of the glaciers that appear as a backdrop to the town. Situated 20 miles farther west in the Beagle Canal than Puerto Williams, Ushuaia is also a naval base, and like all of Argentinian Tierra del Fuego, a duty free area. Though only 60 miles north of Cape Horn, it is fast becoming a tourist centre for South Americans, attracting about 20,000 tourists a year.

In Ushuaia we met an Argentinian/Irish fellow, Manuel Garrido and his stalwart, salt-hardened friend, Oscar Cariui—both of whom had been born and raised in the sailing ships of this area. Manuel spoke faultless English, though he had never been to an English-speaking country; but Oscar spoke only Spanish. Manuel's father had been a sealer and he, as a lad, had accompanied his father on expeditions as far as Antarctica, and often engaged in illegal or sabotage operations. He told us of the time he and his father blew up the fuel storage tanks in Puerto Williams, the charred remains of which are still visible today. With the aid of a small boat and high-powered rifles, muffled by loaves of bread round the barrels, they blew up the tanks and escaped by leaving huge logs camouflaged with kelp, to foul the propellers of the pursuing gunboats.

On the other side of the cement pier where we were moored, an old derelict schooner lay. Manuel explained that it had once been used in illegal sealing operations, which could only be carried out at night or in the worst of weathers when the patrol boats would not be looking for them. This required great seamanship, for the schooner had to come close to the rocks under sail alone, launch a boat, row to the land, capture the seals and return again—while in the most hazardous weather conditions.

•　　　•　　　•　　　•

Lapataia Bay, inside the narrow entrance of the Beagle Canal, opened before us as a labyrinth of islands and bays. At what we thought was the end of the fjord, a narrow opening appeared barely wide enough for *Carronade* to squeeze through. By using our echo sounder, we wound through a further maze of islets and dropped anchor in what surely must be the most secure, protected, and least known anchorage in the world.

Near by, situated between two cordillera-like sections of the Darwin Ranges, was a lake about 30 miles long, and at the head of the lake a hotel run by the director of Tierra del Fuego National Park. We found it rather odd to find one of South America's most exclusive hotels 60 miles from Cape Horn. The hotel was closed for the winter, and the atmosphere casual—fortunate for us, for in our woollen caps, salt-encrusted heavy sweaters and sea boots we hardly looked like normal tourists. A Uruguayan university student working at the hotel acted as guide and interpreter. He took us trout fishing on the lake where ducks and wild geese swam; and before daybreak, guided us on a mountain climbing expedition to a vantage point where we looked down on the Beagle Canal. We could also see one of the rare animals of the world—a guanaco. It is similar to the llama, and the former Tierra del Fuegan Indians used its skin as clothing and as covers for their crude houses. That morning we sat on top of an ice-covered peak and ate breakfast of bread, corned-beef and raisins, while below we saw where the tree line began and the beautiful copper-red leaves of the Arctic birch trees fanned out to lose themselves in the yellows and greens of the lower slopes.

Our plan had been to go as far as the Garibaldi Glacier and anchor at the foot of the cracking, growling cliff of ice. However, where the Beagle Canal branched into two arms the wind funnelled from two directions, doubling the intensity at the very fork. Try as we may with tack after tack, we could not gain way. An approaching snow squall ultimately aided our decision to turn back and run for Ushuaia.

●   ●   ●   ●

Our last call in the channel was at Port Harberton, still marked on the British charts as a refuge for shipwrecked seamen. The Goodalls, descendants of the first European missionary to settle in Ushuaia, live here. In the protected anchorage of the port they moor their yacht—30 years old, of steel construction, with two powerful diesel engines—and use it for ferrying sheep from their island in the channel and for travelling to Ushuaia when their single-engined aircraft is not working. They gave us home-grown lettuces, cabbages, carrots and turnips as well as fresh cheese and jam made from local wild berries. The Goodalls' home was filled with maritime relics collected by the family and resembled a museum. The powerful radio transmitter that Tom Goodall built was used to contact Ushuaia and the Falkland Islands daily. It was amusing to hear Tom speak with the Falklands: "Yes, John, the boys have arrived . . . they took three tacks to get up the harbour, whereas Edward last year took only two."

The Reverend Thomas Bridges, the first settler, came to Patagonia as a missionary and spent much time teaching the Indians farming. He then asked permission to form a mission that was not dependent on charity. Permission was refused, so he resigned. But over the years he greatly assisted the Indians and could speak their language and was respected by them. The Argentinian Government offered him 50,000 acres of unoccupied land anywhere in Argentina. He chose Harberton, continued his study of the Indian tribes, and wrote a dictionary of their language. His son, Lucas Bridges, carried on his work and wrote a book about the Indians of Tierra del Fuego, *The Uttermost Part of the Earth*.

Tom's mother told us tales about the old days and how it was the job of the Indian women to dive for the shellfish, which were the main diet of the people. Mounds of these shells still remain, encircling the flat area where their rough shelters once stood. By digging through these mounds it is possible to find relics made from bone and stone that were used in the everyday life of these people. Little else remains of the former inhabitants. Apparently, there are only 20 full-blooded Indians left in Tierra del Fuego.

One amazing thing about the Indians is that they wore no clothes, despite the biting cold. I recall a most interesting story about Reverend Bridges. He once took a pair of trousers to an Indian who was naked and collecting shellfish beside the canal. The Indian accepted the trousers, bent down and used them to wrap up his day's catch. Bridges protested that they were for him to wear and not to be used for gathering shellfish, for he surely must be cold. The Indian stood up, and looking straight at the heavily clothed Bridges, asked him if his face was cold. Bridges said it wasn't and then the Indian calmly answered ''I am all face''.

Our last anchorage before proceeding to Buenos Aires was at Bahia Aguirre along the southern coast of Tierra del Fuego, 15 miles from the Straits of Le Maire. There we remained a day, weather-bound by a gale and heavy snowfalls. It had once been quite a large settlement, and from the boat we could see an old abandoned sealing works—but the weather wouldn't allow us to go ashore.

The weather seemed too heavy to tackle the straits, so we battened hatches, blocked off all vents, and lit our pressure lamp to serve as a heater. We snuggled up in our bunks to read, with woolly blankets about our ears. With my knees drawn up to my chin, I felt very warm and took great delight in hearing the intermittent thuds of ice that had built up on the spreaders toppling to the deck.

The following morning as we made our way towards the famed Le Maire Straits, the sunrise resembled a giant inferno—a grim reminder and farewell from Tierra del Fuego, the Land of Fire. We passed the forbidding coast—black, devoid of vegetation, with snow-lined cliff crevices—and with the advantageous current *Carronade* averaged 12 knots. The land rapidly dropped astern and I felt relieved to be going, though I wouldn't have missed the experience for the world. And so we left behind the land, capes, canals and islands that were once our dream and headed north to where the flying fish skitter and the warm sea sparkles.

•　　　•　　　•　　　•

Buenos Aires was reached without incident and the trip north was rather anticlimactic after the drama of rounding the Cape. However, in no other city in the world did we receive hospitality such as we were shown there. *Carronade* was only the second Australian yacht to visit Buenos Aires since 1948, and for the six weeks we spent there we were invited out for dinner almost every evening. Day and night, boatloads of visitors swarmed our decks.

Rodolfo Laffranchi, Managing Director of a plastics company, repaired our fibreglass spray dodger at no charge because he had always dreamed of making a voyage such as ours. He felt that by this gesture some part of him would go with us.

While *Carronade* was out of the water it was common for the carpenters to call us for lunch and for us to find that they had brought us meat and fresh bread. An open fire would be going in the boatshed and we would cook our own meat over it. With a lump of juicy meat in one hand and bread in the other we ate heartily and drank from a leather wine sack each time it was passed round. We were greatly embarrassed many times when buying provisions to find one of these workmen insisting on paying for them out of their own very meagre earnings. To have protested at this generosity would have seemed a direct affront. One way and another it was an unforgettable experience in the Argentinian capital.

•　　•　　•　　•

The 3rd of July was Andy's birthday. At midnight, as was the custom aboard *Carronade,* we drank a tot of rum to celebrate. Before retiring again we set the big spinnaker, but it carried away the halyard block at the masthead. So, replacing it with the genoa, we again sought our bunks feeling a little disgruntled, despite a landfall at Rio de Janeiro.

All our navigation along the South American coast was celestial, for Brazil, like most countries of this vast continent, is not well charted. It is interesting to note our chart markings:

> According to the latest determination by the Brazilian Government, the geographical position of Santa Maria Grande Light is . . .

> Because this particular coast has been inadequately surveyed, mariners must proceed with caution.

However, at daybreak the land appeared—silhouette upon silhouette. On top of Corcovado Mountain stands the Cristo Redentor, the huge statue of Christ, glinting in the early morning sun. Ahead the fabled Sugar Loaf Mountain juts out above the heavy mist. Suddenly there was a strong odour in the air. What we first thought to be mist was a watery yellow smog and soon all we could see was Corcovado and Sugar Loaf striving to keep their heads above the choking, polluted air.

The city of Rio de Janeiro (January River), has a population of approximately five million. Its correct name is São Sebastião do Rio Janeiro. Rio was discovered by accident when Goncalo Coelho, a Portuguese mariner blown off course, made a landfall at the mouth of Guanabara Bay on 1st January, 1502. The Huguenots established primitive settlements, which were eventually taken over by the Portuguese. Rio came to life when gold and diamonds were discovered in Minas Geraes, and developed into a flourishing port. In 1763, Rio succeeded Bahia and became Federal Capital of Brazil until 1960 when it gave way to Brazilia. Rio is now the capital of Guanabara State; a separate state of Rio de Janeiro also exists, with its own capital at Niteroi across the bay. (Guanabara comes from the Indian phrase "bay like the sea".)

As we ghosted into the harbour, passing close to Sugar Loaf Mountain we forgot the smog and looked forward to seeing the legendary Rio. Probably the most impressive aspect was the temperature—our first taste of the tropics since Tahiti. At midday we came alongside in a tiny land-locked harbour, man-made and belonging to the Rio Yacht Club. We made our stern lines fast to highly polished bronze rings cast in the form of laid rope.

Rio de Janeiro and Niteroi are twin cities flanking each shore of Rio's scenic harbour. Niteroi, in contrast to its giant sister, is a small town with little or no industry. There is a local saying: "The best thing about Niteroi is the view it has of Rio de Janeiro." To my mind, however, the best thing about Niteroi was its quiet and friendly atmosphere.

Tucked away in the corner of Guanabara Bay was a small British sailing club, resembling an old colonial home with its spacious veranda shaded by drooping chestnut trees. Brazilians have never been a seafaring people and any yachting at this club was purely incidental. The customs official led us to an office, and behind the desk hung a huge oil painting showing two yachts flying colourful spinnakers. However, the two boats were running towards each other—according to the laws of nature this is impossible.

In Brazil there are only two classes, the very rich and the very poor. It is a curious thing, but we noticed that the rich seemed completely oblivious of the pitiful slums in and behind their city. They pretended they did not exist and certainly none of them thought anything should be done about it.

Rio brought many surprises. We were rudely awakened one morning to a tremendous swell rolling down the bay. This was a protected corner of the harbour. Just what was happening? The bay was a mass of breaking waves, some of them tearing boats from their moorings. We learnt that this was a *resake* (pronounced ha-saka) caused by a southern weather disturbance that pushed a strange swell in through the entrance to the harbour causing rough sea conditions. Bob and I were both seasick. We sat for a long time watching the well-formed waves breaking down the centre of the normally tranquil channels. Instead of feeling sick, why not go surfing? So for the next hour we surfed the great waves, catching good long rides and pulling off just before they crashed over the sea wall and into the club. With head and shoulders out in front booming down the face of waves, we surfed screaming with joy "Rio de Janeiro—the best harbour in the world . . . for surf".

Topographically, Rio appeared the most beautiful city in the world to us

26

from the boat—but on stepping ashore the illusion was shattered. Our first impressions of bustling downtown Rio were of noise, dust, beggars, modern skyscrapers, inefficient transport systems, and dazzling dark-eyed girls—some who seemed to be a mixture of every race on earth. It amazed us that magnificent colonial mansions rub shoulders with heart-breaking favelas, the name given to the slum areas built on the mountainside, without water, sanitation, electricity or garbage disposal.

The only advantage these favela dwellers had was the tropical climate. I saw women washing clothes in putrid streams that were mere trickles. Gigantic piles of stinking fly-infested garbage, pigs, starved dogs, shaggy goats, and over-crowded houses constructed of mud, fruit boxes and flattened tin cans were commonplace; but worst of all, the deplorable lean-tos amid scattered garbage piles, hoards of flies and sewage tributaries; these people seemed to have lost all hope for a better life. The favela dwellers were not only negro; I saw many white faces among the lounging, jeering groups perched on broken-down adobe walls beside the road. The bloated bellies and disease-ridden children told a sad story of people battling against impossible odds. Saddest of all, landslides occur during the rainy season in January and February burying thousands of favela dwellers beneath tons of earth and debris.

One hot morning we were awoken suddenly by a rough Australian voice: "Hey you . . . Aussies, get out of the bunk". Next minute the "voice" was aboard. "Tom Harrison is the name." We introduced ourselves and on shaking hands I noticed how like a real worker's hands his were—strong and calloused like rough bark. He was perhaps the toughest man any of us had ever seen—about fifty, heavily muscled, barefooted, rough and unkempt. Tom Harrison, mercenary in the Congo for 18 months, fighter, killer, soldier-of-fortune, crocodile hunter, diver, dam builder, shearer, man of the land, once a family man, and now wanderer for six years across two oceans. This man was in every sense of the word an adventurer.

We adjourned to his boat, *Sundowner,* 24 feet long, white with black trim and a huge ungainly deck house amidships. It had a small white mast and was gunter rigged. Rubbish was strewn all over the deck, and below was worse. On one bunk lay a rotten leather suitcase and hobo-type clothes; on the other a dirty pale blue blanket. We sat down where we could and I almost crushed a photograph of an ugly black-girl—the inscription on the back read "Belle of Badu". Everything was filthy except the small gas stove, which was spotless. Cans, boxes, sacks and dog-eared photo albums lay in a heap. On the shelf just inside the hatch a battered sextant case, navigation books and some grimy jars and coffee-stained plastic cups were strewn. Up forward lay a pile of sails and a ship's clock and compass taken from an aircraft seized while on a raid in the Congo. There was also a typewriter looted from the American Embassy—"My mate beat me to the gold in the safe."

Ten o'clock in the morning, and Tom took his plastic mugs from the shelf and insisted on our having a drink with him. All South American countries have their particular brand of firewater and in these horrible plastic mugs was

Brazil's equivalent—*cachaza*. As we forced down some of this vile liquid we began to learn a little about Tom Harrison, once Tshombie's personal bodyguard and right-hand man to mercenary leader, Mad Mike Hoare.

The next day Tom woke us early, after rowing across from Guanabara Bay. His hair was cut, his face was clean-shaven, and he wore a clean blue shirt and new shorts—though still barefooted. He told us that in the past few days' bad weather a yacht had broken its moorings and drifted down upon his boat at night. He rescued the vessel making it fast to his stern, and then proceeded to strip it of everything valuable: sails, chronometers, and barometers. With yacht stripped, as fortune would have it the wind changed, so he set it adrift. The following day he made a present of his entire "catch" to a young Brazilian couple who were short of finance and having trouble fitting out their boat. "So few Brazilians have the guts to go to sea; I thought they needed a break."

Somehow the conversation swung round to our finances. I was completely broke. As a spontaneous gesture, he reached into his pocket and hauled out a fistful of notes saying "Well, I gotta coupla spare quid you can have . . ." I tried to refuse but he ignored me and began relating the story of how he arrived in Recife from South Africa without a penny in his pocket, and how he was made welcome and taken in by the locals.

"I'd just come from Asuncion Island with about 600 kilos of scrap brass in the bilge. I still had some of the gold with me looted while I was a mercenary in the Congo. I couldn't sell the gold or the brass so I decided to leave. The yacht club gave me a present to be opened at sea. They told me it was a knife . . . but it wasn't; it was $100 U.S. Then I felt pretty bad about the dud cheques I had cashed. I bought a fishing net with some of the money to make a living for myself in the little ports farther south—you may as well have the rest of it. Don't thank me. You might see someone else in trouble one day; you pass it on to them."

I couldn't understand him—a Robin Hood: a man who robbed from the rich and gave to the poor. A man who one day would loot and the following give you the shirt off his back. We talked of Cape Horn and he informed us of his intention of making a rounding.

Two years later Bob Nance wrote to me: "Tom Harrison . . . arrived in Uruguay late spring. He had injured himself and was unable to come ashore for a week after his arrival. Spent only a short time there, was provisioned by the locals as he had no cash and sailed direct for the Falkland Islands. The supply vessel *Darwin* when nearing Port Stanley saw a small yacht anchored near the coast with sheets and boom trailing in the water. Ten minutes passed before he had the strength to drag himself on deck in response to the ship's siren. He did not have the strength to get his anchor up for them to tow him so eventually let it go to the bottom. He worked several months in the Falklands and in May left for Cape Horn. No word was heard from him again. The people of the Falklands tried to talk him out of going but he would always say, "Better a coffin with port holes".

In the goldrush days many a gold-carrying clipper ship laid its bones at the foot of the Cape, and now we believe Tom Harrison and his little sloop *Sundowner* with a bilge full of gold has joined his seafaring forefathers.

After an uneventful passage from Rio de Janeiro, we dropped anchor in Bahia at 3 a.m. one still morning in September. The day dawned hot but was soon cooled by the welcome trade wind. This was our first glimpse of one of the most fascinating ports of call in South America. Beyond a Bahian schooner drifting near by lay a pebbly beach, where several quaint sailing vessels known as "saveiros" prepared to put to sea. They were loaded with wood, furniture, manioc, melons, and women and kids. As we watched, the crewmen hoisted their lanteen sails and were soon under way to join the other saveiros sailing down the bay. We considered ourselves lucky not to be aground as the tide was low, revealing sand and mud-banks that we hadn't seen before. On the banks, swarms of women and children garbed in old dresses, with turbans round their heads sat or squatted in the slush trowling away the mud in search of "mariscos", a local shellfish.

Our first chore was to visit the port captain's office. Apparently in Buenos Aires our clearance noted us as "marineros". In Brazil marineros are the low-class servants who do all the menial jobs round the club and look after the various owners' boats. All boat owners have a personal marinero or servant. Gugutu, who typed out our clearance sheet, was amused and overcame the problem by making Bob "immediador" and me "navigador", leaving Andy as "Capitan".

Though officially known as São Salvador de Bahia da Todos os Santos (a lovely name that means the Holy Saviour of the Bay of All Saints), the city is called simply "Bahia" and its inhabitants "Bahianos". Bahia is the fourth largest city in Brazil and was once the capital. Seventy per cent of its one million inhabitants are negro or mulatto. An unusual feature of the city is that it is built on two levels, with an elevator conveying commuters from the lower to the upper city. It is said to be the oldest city in Brazil, discovered by Amerigo Vespucci in 1501. The architecture of Bahia is old colonial Portuguese; and Bahia is sometimes referred to as the "city of churches" for there is supposed to be one for every day of the year—some more than 400 years old and spectacularly ornate with solid gold and rosewood carvings. The whole town has an atmosphere of a religious museum—antique, unspoiled, eternal.

This was our first stop-over (after seven months in South America) away from the influence of the Western world. Bahia is African-Brazil; we could well have been in Africa. The sights, smells and noises of Bahia seemed to have crossed from one continent to another—from West Africa to Brazil. Everything can be traced to an African origin. One of the beaches is called "chega-negro", which means "the beach of the arrival of the negroes". Christian and African forms of worship seem to merge. There are at least a thousand places of Voodoo worship. Popular deities include the formidable "Yemanja", the Goddess of the Sea—a well-known figure in Nigerian mythology. A good luck charm used by almost everybody is the "figa" shaped like a hand, which wards off the evil eye and brings good luck. Another curiosity is the "berimbau" a musical instrument of African origin. It consists of a bow with an iron string, a hollow gourd, and a coin with which the bow is stroked. In every corner women sell a favourite African dish called "Acaraje"—heavy cakes fried in palm oil on tin stoves.

29

About forty yards from our anchorage floated a gourd used as a buoy for a fishing line, with baited hooks placed at two-metre intervals. Each morning with the incoming tide, an old fisherman sailed or rowed up to the gourd, hauled in the line, changed the bait, then drifted off with the wind. Each day he spent at least an hour watching over his gourd and line. He was a wizened old man with kind, deep-set eyes and a stubbly grey beard, wearing an old broad-brimmed felt hat to protect him from the sun. His movements were slow and calculated; never an ounce of effort was wasted. When the tide was high he put his fishing gear to one side, hoisted his ragged little squaresail, gave us a friendly wave, and set off down the bay.

For weeks we watched the fisherman and not once did he catch a fish. Like Santiago, who fished for 83 days without giving up hope and on the 84th day caught a marlin, the fisherman one morning repeated his ritual and suddenly with speed and dexterity hauled in fish after fish. Satisfied with his day's catch, he sailed slowly down the bay. From his nonchalant manner one would never guess that this day was anything out of the ordinary. This is Bahia: if you catch a fish today you eat well, if you don't, perhaps tomorrow you will have better luck.

Saveiros are quaint sailing craft in which the poor people make a living by fishing or hauling cargo in the Bay of all Saints and along the coast of Brazil. The men who sail them have no idea of the skills they possess or how unusual their vessels are. Originally saveiros were built up to 130 feet long with three masts, but the biggest we saw was about 70 feet. The extraordinary thing about them is that they carry an enormous amount of sail and have no stays whatever on the masts. They are the ultimate in simplicity, with great efficiency and a minimum of gear or expense—modern yacht designers could benefit from the systems they use.

Carronade was anchored on the bend of an inlet where all craft passed as they took the turn; so we were able to study each manoeuvre as the saveiros hardened up on the wind or slackened sheets. The traffic was frightening; at no time of day or night were there less than 20 or 30 sails on the bay. Sometimes in the night we would emerge on deck to find a towering saveiro ghosting past, moving more with the tide than the wind (for the wind drops at night). At other times several lay totally becalmed, stuck on a silvery path to the moon.

When a saveiro is built the builder has no plans, no lines, no measuring rules, but uses a system of "palms"—a boat is said to be so many palms long by so many palms wide. To say the builder has no plans is not quite true. He uses a small flat piece of wood called a "graminho" inscribed with a few crude lines indicating all distances, angles, position of masts, underwater lines, length, beam and draft. It is from this small piece of wood held in the palm of the hand that saveiros have been built for 400 years.

Planks, ribs, keel, horn and stem timbers are all adzed by hand and the lines set by eye. The timber used for the planking and ribs is known as "sucupira", a very heavy hardwood peculiar to Brazil. The masts, which come with many irregular bends, shapes and sizes, are also hardwood but with an elastic quality.

They are actually the cores of trees. When the trees are felled, they are left on the ground so the ants and insects can eat away the outside bark leaving only the rock-hard core. Normally when choosing a suitable mast, the builders select one with a series of bends in the top to facilitate the lead of the throat and peak blocks. Light, cheap canvas is used for sail material and the masts are raked aft so that with little wind the sails will still fill. The sails are deliberately cut in longitudinal sections—all the strain is in a downward direction.

Anti-fouling paint is too expensive, so all bottoms are tarred; and it is traditional to finish with an upward sweep at the bow. Toredo worms are a problem, but deworming the boats is a most interesting operation. Using the tides, the boats are laid on their sides on the beach, and a bed of palm leaves is stacked underneath and ignited. The palm leaves have a high oil content and burn with intense heat. To the untrained eye the boat seems to be on fire, but apparently the method is quite effective, killing the Toredo in their holes. Saveiros were once painted in gay, almost gaudy colours but nowadays the high price of paint prevents this. However, they still use the traditional coloured sails: blues, whites, reds, yellows or a combination of all, making the fleet most spectacular —we even saw one with a leopard-skin panel running down the centre of the mainsail.

Bahia was the first area we visited after leaving Sydney where commercial sail was employed. All transport—both on the bay and to a certain extent along the coast—used sail. At present the Bahianos are poor, but as Brazil progresses they will earn sufficient money to buy engines for their saveiros, and like all historic sailing craft these too will disappear.

The day before we left we made our contribution to maintaining commercial sail on the Bay of all Saints. A thin amiable Bahiano who ran passengers across the inlet where we were anchored always gave his passengers a commentary on the travels of *Carronade*—and they would give us a friendly wave. As he passed each day we caught the same two words "Yate" and "Australianos". We learnt he had 10 children with the 11th on the way. Then one day he was caught in a bad squall that blew his sail to ribbons. He had no money to buy a new one and the boat was his livelihood. So we bought him a new sail. It cost us the equivalent of $8 U.S., but to him this was a fortune. Considering the Brazilian social system, it is debatable whether we did a good thing or not. But we do know that if we had not bought it for him there would have been one less saveiro in Bahia.

We stayed a month in Bahia, savouring its unreal world of the past. It was with reluctance that we poked *Carronade's* bow into the realm of the deep once more and headed north to Barbados.

•   •   •   •

This passage brought a special surprise, an unusual escort—a fish. We slipped our mooring before dawn and ghosted down the channel; and as we cleared the harbour the sun rose and a crimson red heralded a cloudless day cooled by a

31

gentle trade wind. However, we knew this was going to be a hot sticky passage, for the equator runs through the Amazon Basin, and the sun was almost directly over-head.

The sea seemed to be teeming with both bird and sea life. Mother Carey's Chickens fascinated us by their slalom ski-ing motion as they picked up plankton and viscera in our wake. Among the smallest of sea-birds, these sooty-coloured members of the petrel family had long commanded our affection. They never seem to alight on the sea like gulls and other oceanic birds. Forever on the wing, they resort to land only at mating and nesting time. So light and fragile, they run along the water; it is from this habit that they receive their generic name "petrel"—coming from St Peter. In gales we had seen them flitting just above the sea, running down into the troughs of racing waves and fluttering just clear of the foaming crests. Old-time seamen from the Latin nations called them birds of "Mater Cara", which was corrupted by English seamen into "Mother Carey" and the birds were regarded as being divinely protected. On the wing, with their feet just paddling like a runner on the water, they gorged on scraps that we tossed overboard. They never dived for the food or allowed their bodies to touch the sea. "If they gits their wings wet, they drowns" a fisherman once told me.

In contrast, bluebottles (Portuguese Man-O'-War) awkwardly bobbed about on the surface, many of them being thrown aside by our bow wave. They are sometimes called "sailors of the sea" because of a "fin" that acts as a sail; and like many dangerous things in nature, they are extremely beautiful with their mauve bodies, pink sail and crimson tentacles.

One glorious trade wind day, Bob's cry suddenly aroused us. We dashed on deck to see an extraordinary phenomenon—a huge whale jumping out of the water. He would suddenly break the water with a whoosh, his whole body rising vertically into the air, hanging suspended for a moment and then rolling over and hitting the water with a massive splash. The whale kept repeating his act, and we were somewhat alarmed. We did not know which way to run, because each time he surfaced in a different position. We were torn between fascination and fear, and each time he broke the surface the water he shed glistened in the sun, adding to the spectacle. Whales go through these antics to rid themselves of parasites and crustaceans that accumulate on their bodies. A few years ago while cruising the Hawaiian Islands, we saw whales come close into the shallows and roll round on the sand and rock bottom to rid themselves of parasites—but here there were no shallows. We passed a nervous night wondering whether Willy (as we nicknamed him), would drop in on us; but by morning he was gone.

While breakfasting we discovered several rotten eggs and nonchalantly threw them overboard. They had barely hit the water when something darted out and gobbled them up. "Did you see that?" Andy exclaimed. "Something under the boat," I replied. Bob brought out some more rotten eggs and I threw them over. This time we saw that it was a sucker fish, more correctly known as a remora. These fish normally attach themselves to sharks, sea turtles or whales, but they

32

have been known to fasten onto the bottom of small ships. They are scavengers and live on left-over food or garbage. So this is what "Willy" had dumped on us—a sucker fish.

At first we regarded him as a "damn parasite", but as the days passed he stayed with us and we came to look upon him as a regular crew member—and we christened him "Sven". Each morning we would lean over the rail and talk to him as one would to a domestic animal. "Sven, battery acid and cotton wool are not particularly conducive to one's digestion . . ." There was something strangely comforting about having him down there.

On the seventh day out from Bahia, we "crossed the line" for the third time since leaving our homeland, having covered 951 miles in that week. We had a customary celebration dinner and toasted the passing of yet another famous cape—Cabo de São Roque, the easternmost point of South America and the turn of Brazil. It was not long, however, before we ran into the doldrums—that cursed wind belt that runs round the centre of the globe—and wondered if Sven would stay with us when the wind dropped.

The following day Carronade wallowed in an oily calm (Paddy's Hurricane) with stinking hot, listless conditions. During the morning watch I felt like a blob of jelly, barely able to hold the tiller, and down below was worse—bedding and sleeping bags were greasy with salt, perspiration dripped off us and Carronade became a 30-foot sauna bath. The sun was so high over-head, the noon sight became difficult—the sextant readings were 89.2 degrees above the horizon. The air was ominously still and the sky was full of tortured cloud shapes. As usual in the calms, the slatting and banging (known as the "Devil's Orchestra"), nearly drove us mad; so in order to spend the least time in the doldrums we steered a more northerly course. Bob repeatedly related how his brother had once taken 18 days to get through these same doldrums.

This run along the Brazilian coast was one we had looked forward to for some time because of its advantageous current of up to 60 miles in 24 hours. This meant that Carronade could average 200 miles a day with ease if there was wind. Imagining that Sven the remora was no longer with us, we completely forgot him for the remainder of the passage.

It is curious how the simplest venture brightens up an ocean passage. All the flannel lining in my sleeping bag had long ago worn through, and the stuffing fallen to the bottom. I took a childlike delight in throwing it overboard and watching it disappear in our wake. Then I went berserk throwing over old shorts, shirts and a mildewed suit, all previously kept for sentimental reasons—the more I threw over the happier I became. One afternoon at the change of watch a dragon fly landed on deck. After referring to the chart, we calculated he was 400 miles off the coast. Africa was over 2,000 miles away so he must have come from Brazil, flying against the trades. According to the books, this is not possible.

On the 18th day, we raised the island of Barbados with its low green slopes sprawling before us. We rounded the point, sailed into Carlisle Bay and dropped anchor in torquoise water. While waiting for the customs and immigration officials, Andy donned a mask and snorkel and dived over the side to inspect the bottom for weed growth. The bottom was clean . . . but there was Sven. So we all grabbed our masks and dived down to see him. On close examination we found he had welt marks across his back, obviously where he had been hit by the propeller. Poor chap, he had suspicious little eyes and his mouth kept opening and shutting. Cautiously we approached him, patted him on the head, and after we saw he was not frightened began to pull his tail. At the same time we fetched some bread and sardines to feed him by hand. The bread was a huge success, but unfortunately the sardines dissolved before we could get them to his mouth. We now regarded him as one of the family and often when people came to visit we would ask them if they would care to see our pet fish who lived "downstairs".

A brisk breeze and a great spinnaker run brought us from Barbados to St Georges, Grenada, a land-locked harbour where the water is a murky green-brown colour. A narrow channel has been blasted in through the coral, giving access to the inner harbour. How, we wondered, would Sven take to this taste of civilisation? Shortly after dropping anchor we checked to see if he was still there. Sven had gone. He was wise, I guess, to seek clearer water and new pastures. In all, Sven had been with us six weeks, had changed hemispheres, and had travelled over 2,800 miles.

•   •   •   •

It was with regret that I too, left *Carronade* in Grenada, saying farewell and setting out to go my own way in the world. Andy and Bob continued on *Carronade* north to Miami, where they also split up. Bob travelled to England and joined Miles and Beryl Smeeton on their 49-foot ketch *Tzu Hang* for another Cape Horn rounding, from east to west this time—to become the first man to sail round both ways in a yacht. Andy skippered an ocean racer competing in East Coast and Great Lakes events and returned to Florida by sailing inland down the entire length of the Mississippi River. And I joined the 143-foot Canadian schooner *Bluenose* and headed north to Nova Scotia.

34

TYPE: Two-masted Grand Banks schooner. COUNTRY: Canada. OWNERS: Oland &
Sons Ltd, Halifax. YEAR OF CONSTRUCTION: 1963. BUILDERS: Smith & Rhuland,
Lunenberg, Nova Scotia. DESIGNER: William Roue. DIMENSIONS: Overall length
143 feet; water-line length 112 feet; beam 27 feet; draught 15 feet 10 inches.
DISPLACEMENT: 285 tons. SAIL AREA: 10,901 square feet. RIG: 8 sails. HEIGHT OF
MAINMAST: 127 feet. LENGTH OF MAIN BOOM: 84 feet. ENGINES: 2 x 180 H.P.
Caterpillar diesels. CREW: 13.

THE WAKE OF THE BLUENOSE

The West Indies and north to Halifax in a 143-foot schooner

"The wood ain't growin' yet that can beat the *Bluenose*"—Captain Walters.

Lunenburg, Nova Scotia, is a picturesque little town and was once the base
port for the famous Grand Banks fishing fleet. Today, men who once dory-fished
sit in rocking chairs on verandas overlooking the sea, reliving the days that were.
Some are brash and loud while others betray no hint of the tempestuous life
they faced almost daily. No matter which way you look at it, theirs was the
toughest life on any sea. They fished summer and winter alike and then would
race for home to fetch the best price for their catch.

"Grand Bankers" were invariably built for speed, and it was not unusual to
see friendly competition among fishermen. Then in 1919 the Americans issued
the Canadians with a challenge for an annual fishermen's trophy to be run
over seven races. The first series held in the autumn of 1920 went to the United
States. However, a group of Nova Scotian businessmen did not take this defeat

lightly and asked famed designer W. J. Roue to create a schooner that would be fast and also a good carrier.

Thus *Bluenose* was born. She spent her first season on the Grand Banks and in 1921, under the command of Captain Angus Walters, won the International Fishermen's Trophy from the Gloucester schooner *Elsie*.

For the next 17 years *Bluenose* reigned undefeated. The United States made many attempts to regain the trophy, but in vain. They even built specially light racing schooners and sent them on a couple of trips to the Banks so they would qualify, but still could not toss the champion. In 1938 the last series was held. 17 years of hard fishing had taken their toll yet Captain Walters in *Bluenose* again took the series from his old rival Ben Pine and the *Gertrude L. Thebaud*. No one knows what made *Bluenose* so fast. Some say it was the wood, others say a freak in building and others that it was her skipper.

For years the jealous men from Massachusetts complained that *Bluenose* was not a true fishing boat, but their claims were empty—they simply could not build a boat to beat her. And they should not have felt so bad, because the Canadians were unable to do so either. Roue later designed *Halegonian* with the avowed purpose of topping his famous design. He failed.

However, racing was only a spectacular sideline for *Bluenose*. Basically she was a "banker" or fishing boat. Her record catch of 600,000 lb of salt cod still stands. She carried a crew of 26, including 16 dorymen, who worked from dawn till dusk fishing in weather so cold they soaked their hands in sea water to warm them up; and in the back of their minds was the continual fear that the schooner might not find them at dusk if the weather shut in. Many lost dorymen lent weight to this fear.

In 1939 with the outbreak of war, *Bluenose* was sold to the West Indies as a banana boat, and ended her days in 1946 when blown ashore in a hurricane off Haiti. *Bluenose* had sailed her way into maritime history and into the hearts of her countrymen. Today, her memory is perpetuated on one side of the Canadian dime.

The legend was reborn in 1963 when the brewing firm of Oland & Sons had *Bluenose II* built. The original plans were used, the same firm of Smith and Rhuland and many of the old shipwrights built her, and a few of the old crew were on hand to offer advice, including 82-year-old Captain Angus Walters and 84-year-old designer, Bill Roue. She was commissioned in late 1963 as a goodwill ambassador for Nova Scotia and its seafaring traditions. To avoid the severe northern winter she goes south to charter in the Caribbean. That is where I met her in January 1968 in St Georges, Grenada, British West Indies. I was fortunate indeed to be accepted as one of the fo'c's'le hands.

On a warm, bustling Saturday evening in the Carenage, *Bluenose* lay stern to the quay, tall topmasts reaching into the sky, the surrounding hills dotted with lights; the Nutmeg Bar was in full swing, and the rhythm of a steel band echoed across the basin. I stood on the quay and waited for the ship's tender to pick me up. As we passed beneath the stern I could, in the clear night, read the huge gold-embossed words:

BLUENOSE II
LUNENBURG, N.S.

I picked up my belongings and moved forward to the fo'c's'le. That night I lay in my bunk taking in my new surroundings. I could not help being amused. I looked anything but a sailor, coming aboard at midnight and in place of the traditional seabag I carried all my belongings in two cardboard cartons and a plastic garbage bag. My bunk was upper forwardmost in the fo'c's'le, and as I dosed off I caught strains of conversation . . . "Yeah, that was when my old man was rum runnin'" . . . "remember the time we went into Halifax doin' sixteen with the main boom draggin' in the water?" This life will do me I thought.

The majority of visitors on a ship like *Bluenose* look in awe at the great masts and complex rigging, imagining her with sails set and themselves at the wheel. I've watched them many a time. They walk round, scan the rig, hold the iron steering wheel for a moment, give it a spoke or two in passing, marvel at the height of the masts (but normally don't realize there are two big topsails bent to the mast doublings), and then are impressed by the modern carpeting, hi-fi sets, pretty pictures and panelling in the saloon for the charter parties. Before they leave they usually take a quick peek down the fo'c's'le hatch with an expression that might read "Oh! I wonder what's down there in that hole?" Were they allowed to descend into that hole, they would find a place of character. Certainly it is not plush like the saloon or passenger accommodation, but it has a charm of its own, with rough finish, big heavy beams, pictures of square-riggers, bunks in tiers and a large mess table. It has a lived-in look: oilskins on hooks, rubber boots on the deck, personal possessions crammed into shelves, unmade bunks, plenty of chatter and yarn spinning. It is the very heart, the throbbing pulse of the ship.

I believe that the happiest and most rewarding days of seafaring are those spent in the fo'c's'le of a vessel like this. Very seldom do men now sleep in tiered bunks in the eyes of a vessel, and I am lucky to have had that experience. Anyone who has not lived in a fo'c's'le, cannot know exactly what it is like.

The fo'c's'le is a home-away-from-home for the men who live there. It was very often the only home they ever knew in the old days. A seaman's bunk is not just a place to lie down. It is his private place, and, by the seaman's unwritten code, no one would dare interfere with another's bunk or the possessions lying on it. It gives you a great sense of security to be lying in your bunk estimating the speed of the vessel by the pressure being exerted against you, forcing you into the clothing rack as you stare at the big beams overhead and look round the cabin, to see your shipmates relaxing.

After a hard watch, they are bleary eyed and unshaven; they have turned in fully clothed and crusted with salt, but you know all along that these men, though lost in sleep at the moment, would spring to life at an "All Hands!" call. Then you would work shoulder-to-shoulder with them on the bowsprit, fisting heavy wet canvas one minute, only to need both hands for yourself the next to hang on as the bowsprit buries waist deep in the shock of icy water, and to have the sail torn free to flog like a wild thing in the screeching gale. Finally, the sail secured, you would turn in again and take a second look at those out-stretched men, suddenly realizing why the brotherhood of the sea exists.

The vessel is commanded by the Master at the stern. Orders are conveyed to the crew by the Mate, and sometimes through the Bosun (a man caught between the devil and the deep; neither an officer nor crew member), but it is these fo'c's'le dwellers who perform the actual tasks of setting sail, overhauling the rigging, and scraping and painting—not to mention other chores such as cleaning bilges, scouring and scrubbing, and emptying garbage.

For all this however nature rewards them tenfold, and even though, contrary to what romantics believe, most days at sea are pure misery, those days which are good are so grand they compensate for the others. As time passes we forget the bad and remember the good, and as further time passes we imagine that it was all good.

Bluenose II was commanded by Captain Ellsworth Coggins (ex-master of the *Bounty*). He had a remarkable record at sea. In 1931, when he was barely 19 and was serving as seaman aboard a three-masted schooner, the captain fell ill and died. Coggins then slid up a notch and became the bosun. The mate who had assumed command was washed overboard shortly afterwards and lost. The man who had shipped as bosun (who had become mate) took over only to become disabled through illness. That left Coggins in command of the ship, which he navigated home safely. Says he "I went through every post on that ship from seaman to master in a month and a half." He was awarded master's papers in sail when only 23.

An incident that I like to recall occurred when heading "down islands" in the Caribbean. We had set every stitch of canvas *Bluenose* could carry, and with a brisk beam breeze we were "honking rightalong". Approaching from the opposite direction was the replica of the *America*, a lovely 106-foot schooner built by an American brewing firm. This magnificent spit and polish schooner— capable of a good turn of speed under the prevailing sailing conditions—was under power.

The age-old animosity was still there. Her crew regarded *Bluenose* as a rough fishing schooner and on a previous occasion had refused us permission to inspect their vessel. On the other hand we looked upon them as yachtsmen blundering their way round the islands on a real sailing vessel that was alien to them.

That day as *America* came abeam, Captain Coggins was leaning on the rail by the wheelbox, his eyes fixed on her bare masts. He turned round, took the cigar out of his mouth and said to us all . . . "She looks like a plucked chicken, don't she?"

It was well into May when *Bluenose* sailed north from the West Indies towards Halifax, her home. I remember one night on the homeward passage between

38

the Virgin Islands and Bermuda. Jim Bell, another crew member, and I had just come off watch, and the whole crew was lounging on deck by the fo'c's'le hatch, a half empty case of beer against the bulwarks. I joined them, stretching out on deck and resting my head on a rag beneath the gypsy of the windlass. (The rag smelled of linseed oil.)

Later I recorded in my log. "The only light is the one from the fo'c's'le companionway, delicately outlining the immediate features of the ship. We can't see the helmsman, but beyond the stern the Southern Cross lies low on the horizon. Tomorrow the Cross will be gone.

"Every now and then someone lights a cigarette, illuminating faces and hands in the night. You recognize the face for an instant and then it disappears, leaving only the glowing red tip, which becomes brighter each time he inhales.

"This night is perfect. The ship's head pointed towards the North Star, the Atlantic to ourselves, the tall schooner snoring along at seven or eight knots and a phosphorescent bow wave on an inky black sea . . ."

And I remember too, the most unlikely of us saying in a barely audible voice, "Look at the anchor and bow silhouetted against the path of the moon. There is real beauty this night."

Another great time aboard a sailing vessel is meal-time. Some of my fondest memories of *Bluenose* are of bounding off the deck to the mess table, rushing for the best seat and bellowing for the cook. Sea cooks have always had it tough, but Kenny — cook on the *Bluenose* — had his hands full with us. Out of pure fun, it was the custom to come down, bellow at him and make uncomplimentary remarks about his cooking even before you knew what it was. He would fire back his favourite Jamaican curses, blasting us to the end of the earth and telling us we never had it so good. Then he would serve the food out and say "Pick op, mon". As we wolfed our food the yarns would begin.

•   •   •   •

Between Bermuda and Halifax there were winds and seas which forced us to heave-to under foresail and lashed helm. But there was no hint of that the first day out of Bermuda. We got under way early in the morning. The four lowers (main, foresail, jumbo and jib) were set fast and efficiently for this was the run home. About noon there was an "All Hands" call for the jib-topsail. It was a sunny winter's day and the sun felt warm on our backs. *Bluenose* was making ten knots and the crew was keen and alive. A man sprang to the weather foot-rope to loose the gaskets. There was a man a piece for the halyard and winch, and way aft along the leeward rail six men swayed to the sheet. The sail flogged itself aloft, booming like a cannon, and the mast twisted under the might of the big flogging sail. Already the ship was surging a knot faster under the added pressure; the helmsman put the helm up and the vessel slashed into the wind. Eight men to the sheet now and she came in inch-by-inch and was finally belayed, and *Bluenose* charged north.

Later I recorded: "All my life I dreamed of something like this; a great schooner heavily geared with powerful sails tromping on a sea that is alive with leaping white horses and tumbling crests . . . many imagine but few experience . . . today we are on the port tack, the compass is to starboard. I stand to leeward, steering. I feel the pulse of the ship vibrating through the four-foot wheel, cast in iron from the Lunenburg foundry and raked aft with its shaft aimed halfway aloft; she runs straight and true as if she is in a groove."

That was the afternoon of 19th May; the following morning a series of events exceeded my wildest expectations as to what *Bluenose* could really do. It began at midnight during the Mate's, Mr Skodje's watch with the vessel averaging 16 knots for the four hours until 0400. The anemometer showed 40 m.p.h. At 0300 I was awakened by the increased pressure on the ship. I was being forced into the shelf above my bunk so I knew we were really moving. At 0400 Jim and I were called for watch, and we hurriedly dressed and emerged on deck as the Mate called all hands to take in the jib-topsail. While waiting for the remainder of the crew, Jim took the helm with the "old man" (the Captain), while I stayed forward with fellow watchmate, Rick Clow.

I could not believe my eyes. There was a small crescent moon peeping through the racing clouds and the vessel was going so fast the stern caused the seas to break prematurely. What a sight! The ship making 16 knots, three feet of water in the lee rail and big breaking seas keeping endless race with us. The wind increased, the deadeyes went under as she lay down more and more, and the leeward wake was white as far as the eye could see. The night was dark and the schooner thundered along. Now *Bluenose* was making 18 knots or more, with the lee scuppers boiling and the lanyards half under (the anemometer read 60 m.p.h.).

A 143-foot schooner carrying the four lowers and jib-topsail in winds like this; there has never been a vessel built that could withstand such treatment! Something had to go. Since the weakest point was the fore-topmast, the jib-topsail had to come off first. Mike and I took to the bowsprit, hanging on with both hands for ourselves as we dipped in up to our waists. The halyard was released, but the downhaul had to be taken to the winch before the sail would come down. While trying to get a grip on the flailing canvas we were told to forget about the jib-topsail and get the "big patch" (the mainsail) off.

We worked at a feverish pace. The big coiled throat and peak halyards were made ready to run, and the mainsheet put to the winch ready for crutching the boom. The gaskets were down in the lazarette so I jumped down to pass them up to Rick. Suddenly there was a report and a giant tearing noise, and Rick yelled down to me:

"Forget about the rest of the gaskets, the whole jesus main just blew out of the boltropes!"

I looked up. The top of the lazarette made a picture frame round the mainsail as she ripped. Have you ever seen 4,000 feet of canvas go? Huge sections of it were flogging themselves to pieces, and one of the emergency life-raft capsules (weighing 600 lb) was thrown out of its cradle. The noise was defening.

Under foresail, jumbo and jib she continued to make 11 knots, and with the

Bluenose's fine spoon bow gave her a splendid entry

Barrelling along under the benevolent Caribbean sun

Eleven knots under foresail alone shortly after the mainsail blew out of its boltropes
Jamaican cook and steward relaxing on the foredeck

Cleaning a good catch of bonito

Sterling Hayden's former schooner, the magnificent Wanderer, wrecked on Rangiroa
Paradise really exists—Rangiroa Atoll

Andy on the helm of the fated schooner Valrosa
Valrosa at Bora Bora on her final cruise

Bob Nance on the track to Melville's famed Typee Valley

mainboom crutched and the gaff lowered (it looked ridiculous lowering just the gaff) all hands then "muckled onto" the flailing pieces of canvas. It was hard and dangerous work. The bulk of the sail was caught up on the after boom lift on the starboard side and was dragging in the water. Time and time again, we got the heavy canvas aboard, only to have it torn from our hands by the wind. Finally we secured it to the boom in ugly bulky lumps, and Captain Coggins remarked "She's one hard lookin' mess."

The seas kept endless race and the wind screeched. Meanwhile, the jib-topsail sheet block was drumming on the ship's sides and finally beat itself to pieces, tearing the cheeks off the block and leaving only the iron frame and the sheave. Moreover the jib-topsail was still to be furled. We had a tough battle. Being wet, it was twice as heavy as usual, and it took a full fifteen minutes to secure. The end result was anything but a harbour stow.

Daylight came with a grey sky, grey tumbling sea and windstreaks across the faces of the rollers, indicating how hard it was still blowing. This had been quite a morning, but there wasn't a man aboard who didn't look at the vessel with pride and wonder. The expressions on their faces seemed to say: "She's a big hooker, but believe it or not I just saw her do 20-plus knots, a new record. I wonder how the old *Bluenose* would have fared."

Both Captain Coggins and the Mate, Mr Skodje, said later that they had seen her do eighteen before, but never like this. Their view had been from the stern. They said that she was pressed so far down that water was foaming aboard from both sides. In fact her bow was pressed down level with the rushing water, and had something not let go we could have driven her right under.

Jim and I talked about the watch. He and I had once shared the helm at sixteen knots. We remembered that it took two of us to turn the wheel. But when he and the skipper were on the helm during the blow, it took their combined efforts to turn a single spoke.

Mike's below deck experience was interesting. He was rudely awakened when the ship lurched, hit in the face with two *Playboy* magazines, hit in the chest with a turtle shell, and felt a sharp pain in the groin when hit by a flying projectile. On examining it more closely, he found it was a half gallon flagon of Barbados Rum, still intact.

On arrival in Halifax I was paid off. From the shipping office I returned to the ship for the last time to collect my seabag and bosun's tools. I took one last look at the lofty windwagon with her big spoon bow pointed towards the city. At first she was just a replica of a legend; but now with more than 60,000 sea miles under her keel and many experiences of her own (one of which I shared), she has earned her own legend. She is, in my mind, the best and fastest schooner in the world today.

People come from far and wide to see the *Bluenose;* few realize she is not the original. Some critics say "The modern Bluenosers (the nickname given to fishermen from Nova Scotia) do not have it as hard as the old timers out on the Banks." This may be partly true, but they still have their hard times.

Last year on her annual southbound trek to the West Indies, *Bluenose* ran into a gale near Bermuda and took freak seas that washed two seamen overboard. One was recovered; the other lost to the sea. I can picture how those seamen in the fo'c's'le stared at the empty bunk of their late shipmate and wondered how he fared in the bitter fury of the icy sea that night. And the one who made it back, how lucky he must feel!

•　　　•　　　•　　　•

In 1968, the same year I sailed aboard *Bluenose,* Captain Angus Walters passed away. On the morning the skipper was buried, the newspaper ran a story that began "On a kind of day a sailor likes . . . There was a fresh offshore breeze, good visability and warm sun. The Lunenburg wharves were busy with his old trade, as fishermen in woollen mittens handled salt cod ashore from four Newfoundland fishing boats.

"Young lads with red cheeks pushed barrowloads of fish into scarlet painted warehouses and ships' masts fingered the sky between the rooftops. *Bluenose II* lay alongside the wharf. On board her, working crew and officers brushed and pressed their seldom-used best suits before they joined the mourners and townsfolk in tribute."

His death brought to a close the era of the Grand Banks fishermen. However, the tradition he set still lives on in those who sail today aboard *Bluenose II*, and I feel proud to have been a part of it.

The following afternoon *Bluenose II* slipped her mooring and with Captain Ellsworth Coggins in command, sailed out of Lunenburg. Her mainsail cracked like a whip as it was hoisted, then the canvas tightened in the wind. A gull lifted off the shore and followed her down the channel . . . maybe Captain Walters is still watching over *Bluenose*.

SAIL PLAN

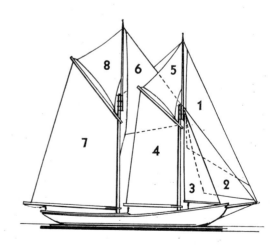

1. *Jib Topsail* . . . .　966 *sq. ft.*
2. *Jib* . . . .　804 *sq. ft.*
3. *Jumbo* . . . .　770 *sq. ft.*
4. *Foresail* . . . . .1,640 *sq. ft.*
5. *Fore gaff-topsail* . . . . .　560 *sq. ft.*
6. *Fisherman's staysail* .1,305 *sq. ft.*
7. *Mainsail* . . . . .4,100 *sq. ft.*
8. *Main gaff-topsail* . . . .　756 *sq. ft.*

TYPE: Two-masted schooner of teak and oak. COUNTRY: Tahiti. OWNER: Marc Darnois. YEAR OF CONSTRUCTION: 1901. BUILDERS: Samuel White, Southampton. DIMENSIONS: Length 99 feet; beam 18 feet; draught 13 feet. TONNAGE: 110 gross. SAIL AREA: 5,000 square feet. RIG: 6 sails. ENGINES: 2 x 671 G.M. diesels. CREW: 5 Tahitians. USE: Charter work in French Polynesia.

WRECK OF THE VALROSA

On an atoll in the Tuamotu Archipelago

Many times I had read of superstitions and of sailors having forewarnings of dangers ahead and, incredible as it sounds, I knew of the coming catastrophe. After leaving Papeete, Tahiti, on a charter to the Tuamotu Archipelago, we had been dogged with bad luck. It was almost as if we were doomed from the start. However, I shrugged off these thoughts, attributing them to natural anxiety from my responsibility as First Mate. So worried was I that I called Dick Johnstone, another member of the crew, and asked him to keep a look-out from the bow. This made me feel easier.

Earlier that night we had sailed from Rangiroa Atoll for Manihi Atoll some 80 miles to the N.E. We received a severe battering from headwinds coupled with the short steep seas. Unknown to us we were caught by a freak set of currents, by no means uncommon to this area, but currents which, before this night was over, would sweep us to destruction upon the coral reefs of Tikehau Atoll. Because of the weather conditions Captain Marc Darnois altered course allowing a safety margin of at least 25 miles to pass well to the north of the Tuamotus. By daybreak, the way would be clear to pass between Tikehau and Matahiva and stand towards the south for Huahine in the Society Islands.

When I think back to the occasion, I remember my thoughts well. I was alone with the helm, the sea and the long heaving deck. A faint white light threw life onto the brass compass and binnacle before me. A fraction west of sou-west was the course. The heavy rain made the varnish work and spars glisten. The air was swollen with freshness and the wind moaned aloft. Up forward the long forefoot snored along, while the foaming seas kept endless race.

At 4.25 a.m. Dick had just gone below after seeing nothing ahead, when suddenly there was the most incredible vision—a flash of white and the silhouette of a coconut tree directly ahead of the bowsprit. It was that same reef that for generations sailors have glimpsed before their destruction. In those few remaining instants you try and imagine what it is going to be like.

I spun the wheel hard'a'starboard and, though I don't remember saying it, yelled to the skipper, Marc Darnois, who was sleeping just inside the after coachhouse, "Marc, Marc, I can't believe it!"

Next I remember the images of dark waves beside the ship, being picked up on the sea, and finally the agonizing crunching and grinding sounds as the vessel came to rest on the coral with the deck towards the shore and the keel to weather. The helm spun like a chocolate wheel as the rudder grounded, sheering off the worm-gear steering and at the same time ejecting the magnificent scroll-work panel into the air like a champagne cork.

At first Marc and I were the only ones on deck. A few streaks of light showed the outline of the stricken *Valrosa* lying over on her side. We knew she was finished.

Marc gave the order to rig a life-line to shore. It was obvious that the 42-ton lead ballast on the schooner's knife-like keel had snapped off on impact, and we had no alternative but to abandon ship.

Fortunately, the night before during bad weather we had put an extra lashing on the main boom, which now enabled us to use the mainsheet as a life-line. Pua, a Tahitian crew member, and I moved aft to unrove it while Henri, the Marquesan engineer went below to fetch distress flares. A huge sea engulfed the ship and we clung to the boom gallows and mainsheet assembly for grim death as a huge wave crashed on us—then another and another. Endlessly they came, and after each we would unrove a little line.

Marc was not so lucky. While setting off a distress flare, he nearly met with disaster when the flare backfired and hit him on the cheekbone.

Then an extraordinary thing happened. Stewardess, Biky Marque, came up on deck clutching a horseshoe and with all her strength, hurled it into the sea. (The day before, we had visited the wreck of the 96-foot pilot schooner *Wanderer*, formerly owned by actor Sterling Hayden. In 1964 after being bought by millionaire Joe Price, the *Wanderer* commenced a world cruise and was bound for Miami when she was wrecked on the south-west tip of Rangiroa Atoll in the Tuamotu Archipelago. Because of her inaccessability, we were among the few people to visit the wreck. As souvenirs Dick and I took a belaying pin each and one of our passengers took a horseshoe that he found tacked just inside one of the hatches.)

Biky later said that when she was awoken with the impact and saw water gushing through the ship, she immediately thought of the horseshoe. She frantically searched amongst the chaos for it and as if exorcising an evil spirit, hurled it into the sea.

With our rubber life-craft, Henri and our Egyptian cook, who had gone absolutely crazy, made a skilful landing onto the treacherous coral shelf, and

44

fastened the life-line to a coral-head. Our four passengers (two had been marooned in similar circumstances several years previously in East Africa) were the first to be ferried ashore. They were followed by Pua, Biky and Dick, leaving Marc and myself still aboard.

We sat together, feet on the lower bulwarks and backs against the deck. The ship was sinking. Slowly the water rose. Past our ankles, knees and finally our waists. Suddenly, alongside Marc, the deck opened up like a giant clamshell and spat planks and fastenings into the sea. The ship's back was broken in just 25 minutes. We knew with the keel gone there was nothing to hold her together, but to see her go this quickly was unbelievable. Marc looked at me and said in English "She is sinking, now we must leave the ship," and as an afterthought "Oh! I love my sextant, get it for me."

It was still dark as we jumped into the sea and swam through the surf to the safety of the coral shelf. The sextant case opened with the impact of hitting the water. I slammed it shut leaving it full of sea-water and waited for a suitable wave. Stalling my body motion upon its crest, I allowed myself to be carried along with the suctioning from the back of the wave. It was an old trick I had learnt from my childhood surfing days, and enabled me to somewhat cushion the impact of slamming into the deadly-sharp coral.

We sat in a line along the sandy beach and helplessly watched the heart-breaking sight of the 100-foot schooner being pounded to matchwood by the heavy seas. It was raining. Towards the east the sun struggled to penetrate the leaden storm clouds, and cast streaks of orange light on our dying ship. We guessed the entire port side had been stoved in as many interior fittings, which we all recognized, began to wash ashore. Oddly enough I found the belaying pin I had taken from *Wanderer*.

The two hefty fisherman anchors mounted on the forward bulwarks slowly tumbled into the sea, and the sails one by one were torn from their spars. I was caught between fascination and horror. We saw before us the tremendous power the sea possessed. Stout oak frames and sturdy teak planks bonded together by great bronze fastenings 62 years previously by Southampton shipwrights were crushed like an egg-shell beneath a falling top-maul hammer. I had a sickly feeling in my stomach, for I had been at the helm and, whether it was my fault or not, it would always live with me. If I had only seen the reef . . . if I had listened to God's warning . . . if it hadn't been raining . . . if the wind had been ahead I may have heard the roar of surf. Can this really be happening? Visions of the distraught Marc Darnois staring at his "life's blood" being destroyed. Biky sobbing into the shawl wrapped round her shoulders. Dick Johnstone, the American crewmember, vainly searching amongst rubble for any of his possessions. Passengers huddled together shivering against the cold and rain. "My God, my God, why did I ever choose to go to sea?"

The grand finale came when, like a dying person trying to get to her feet, *Valrosa's* huge masts lifted high into the air, suddenly dropping with a crash. Again and again they lifted, high and higher still; she was like a living thing playing out the last act. On the fourth time, the masts were thrown clear of the mast steps and the vessel completely dismantled. *Valrosa* was dead.

In just one and three quarter hours there wasn't a piece of wood (except for the long counter stern, which came ashore intact) on the reef I couldn't pick up by hand. Marc was perched on top of the counter stern directing salvage operations. Dressed in a Tahitian pareu and Navy P-jacket he stood balanced on his one leg (his other leg had been lost while in the French Air Force: he was shot down on the last day of the war), the wind and rain lashing his long silver hair and expressionless face. It was as if life had left him, and remaining was only the empty shell. I thought of Coleridge's *Ancient Mariner*.

As most of us were clad only in shorts, we searched the rubble for clothes. I found a pair of swim-fins, cut off the front section, and made a pair of shoes for walking on coral. The remnants of a rubber diving suit made an excellent shirt and helped against the cold. (It was amazingly cold, despite the fact that we were in the tropics.) For food we found pieces of pineapple or apples, some tins of mineral water and even a jar of caviar. By mid-morning there was nothing but a huge pile of timber on the reef and no one had salvaged any personal effects. One of the passengers lost jewellery worth 2,000,000 francs—and carried no insurance.

Tahitians from a near-by copra village aided salvage operations. Curiously though, because the wreck occurred near their village, they believed that everything dragged up the beach automatically belonged to them. The following day, by means of small boats they ferried us the 21 miles across the lagoon to the main village of Tuherahera, where we stayed for the next five days.

The 200 inhabitants of the village banded together to make our stay comfortable. As our rag-clad and deeply tanned "family" hobbled along the wharf, the Tikihauans were fighting amongst themselves as to who was going to look after who. We slept in their beds while they slept on the floor. Dick and I were becoming quite accomplished with the Tahitian dialect and began accompanying the early morning fishing party out to the pass.

We also helped collect copra. Copra is simply dried coconut. The nut is collected, split in halves with an axe, and left to be dried by the sun on sheets of galvanized iron. Once dry, the coconut is gouged away from the husk and bagged to be sent to market, eventually to be utilized in the making of perfumes and oils. Between 11 a.m. and 2 p.m. we took a siesta, when the heat of the day was strongest. In the late afternoon we played volley ball; and after our *tamaa,* the Tahitian meal, we sat beneath a Tou tree with ukuleles made from coconut shells and quietly hummed to a solemn tune that I could not understand but I knew was about the *Valrosa*.

All our money and possessions had been lost, leaving us on the same plane as the Tikihauans themselves. Being shipwrecked on a perfect tropical atoll is usually considered a romantic adventure. But in practice, because our upbringing and culture are so different, we soon tire of this simple idyllic life and long for a book to read or a stimulating conversation. Atolls are either heaven or

46

hell—heaven if you can leave whenever you like: hell if you are obliged to spend the rest of your days there.

One day the small trading schooner *Mahinateata* called at Tikihau. And as we drew away from the atoll, bound once again for Tahiti, Marc said to me: "I had an idea catastrophe would strike the other night. I should learn to listen to God's warnings. The last time I didn't listen I lost my leg, now I've lost my ship."

Upon our arrival in Papeete we had to face the rumours of how we deliberately wrecked the ship for the insurance, of how rotten she was . . . But this is always the way. They said the same of *Wanderer*. Yet we found her after she was pushed 200 yards across a coral shelf and had weathered wind and sea for a year, still intact and showing no signs of rot. "Rotten", they said, "insurance job."

Wanderer, 82 years old; *Valrosa,* 62 years old; wrecked within 50 miles of each other and within one year. But the real tragedy was to have visited the wreck of one of the world's greatest schooners and that very night wreck another.

TYPE: Two-masted schooner of wood. COUNTRY: U.S.A. OWNER: Hugh H. Gordon.
YEAR OF CONSTRUCTION: 1924. DESIGNER: Edsel Schock. DIMENSIONS: Overall
length 60 feet; length on deck 45 feet; beam 14 feet; draught 6 feet. RIG: Main,
fore, working jib, genoa, fisherman staysail, gollywobbler. ENGINE: 451 G.M.
diesel. CREW: 4.

THE SCHOONER MONSOON
—MY FIRST COMMAND

Voyage from Tahiti to Honolulu with a Tahitian crew

Tahiti waterfront was beginning to look dreary, it had now been months since
the wreck. I was now living out in the Fataua Valley and I had learnt much about
the Polynesian people. My small concrete-walled house, which I referred to as
the "country estate", was ideally located beside a river far up the valley amid
lush vegetation. After rain I savoured the rich earthen smell, water ran past the
door in wild torrents, and grey mist kept the valley cool. Eight thousand feet
above, the top of sombre Mount Orophena was encircled by its permanent
mantle of cloud. Formidable walls of basalt descended from the central crater
and fanned out into the profusion of greenery.

The middle of the day was always hot and unpleasant; it was the early mornings
and late afternoons I enjoyed most. In the cool airiness of first light, Dick Johnstone and I would frequently bicycle out to Point Venus to collect the mangoes
that had fallen over-night. The Tahitians adopted the continental custom of
coffee and croissants for breakfast, but with the slight difference. They put

the coffee in a dish, dipping in pieces of bread to make them moist, drained the coffee from the dish with both hands cupped beneath, and finally wiped their mouth with the back of their hands, happily remarking "Ehh! Tamaa matai" — *good meal*. On foot, Dick and I hiked deep into the Fataua Valley, forging high into the clouds till the going became rough with incessant rain showers. Probing where no paths existed, we found miraes (old Polynesian worshipping platforms) and signs of former civilizations. We forded rivers, streams and waterfalls, occasionally stopping to gulp handfuls of cool clear streamwater.

Dick and I were in an unusual position; the authorities refused us permission to work, but on the other hand refused permission to leave Tahiti until our new passports arrived. Dick was the thriftiest person I'd ever met; he could live on 5 to 10 cents a day and knew more tricks than Houdini himself. We body-surfed at the black sand beaches near Tierai and we roamed the small villages on Tahiti-iti. Dick owned a yellow T-shirt, a pair of khaki shorts and a pair of thongs to protect his bandaged feet, which suffered from coral poisoning from injuries received during the wreck. I had a pair of Levi jeans bought for me by the local doctor's wife and a white T-shirt ringed with a couple of red bands. I had no shoes. This was the sum total of our possessions.

Life was magnificently simple; we had no worries; our big decision was what to do each day. From habit we looked round to tidy up non-existent clothes, papers and travelling gear. Our only duty to the French Empire was to report each week to the immigration department to face the same question: "Passports arrived yet?" answer "Non, pas encore", then leave. One of our pursuits was learning the Tahitian language, and so our first possession was a dictionary published by the Mormon Church.

In this time I had noticed a fine little schooner, the *Monsoon,* moored stern-to on the Quay du Commerce. I was surprised one day to receive a message from her new owner asking if I would meet him at a specified time. Hugh Gordon was a senior pilot with Pan American Airways, and after only a short discussion he offered me the job of taking *Monsoon* to Honolulu. Shaking my hand, with a final "Get a crew, get the boat to Honolulu and get it there in good shape . . . I'll be in touch", he was gone. Suddenly I was alone with my first command. It was rather a good feeling not to have to worry about bringing any baggage aboard, for, with the exception of the belaying pin from *Wanderer* I was wearing everything I possessed. And that moment I resolved in the future not to burden my life with material possessions. I had even forgotten exactly what had been lost in the wreck, things which to me before had been almost priceless.

Finding a crew wasn't easy. Dick would have been ideal but he was leaving for Australia—a trip to the States was the last thing he wanted to do at that time. I had plenty of offers from the "milk-run" crowd—those who had rolled down from California, but that was the sum total of their experience. Others, because of the age difference, tried to lord it over me. A guy nicknamed "Alligator Jaws" condescended to offer his services for $500, plus the fare home; someone else informed me that because I was on the *Valrosa* I had no chance of getting through with *Monsoon;* and another asked to see the captain, and when told

49

that I was, he said I was a *"smart Alec"*, and snickered off down the quay. I had to find a crew, and they had to be good men, for if I wrecked *Monsoon,* my name henceforth would be mud.

Meanwhile, Dick helped make *Monsoon* ready for sea. Then one evening, two old friends, Pua and Vanaka, shyly approached me and said "Dass, we want to go to America on the *Monsoon."* Here was my salvation, two of the finest seamen in all French Polynesia: Vanaka Haiti, who had spent 20 years at sea on island schooners and could fix anything by improvisation; and Pua Terooatea, a happy-go-lucky Polynesian who had sailed for 25 years on inter-island schooners and knew the passes of every atoll in the Tuamotus—an invaluable man should we need to run for cover.

Hugh agreed to their repatriation and the harbour master consented to let them leave Tahiti. I had to get Pua a passport and send both their passports to Fiji for American visas. Hugh wrote to me days before departure: "God, I want to do that trip . . . one way or another, I'll be there when the boat sails." This was an enormous relief because I had never had the responsibility of navigating. I knew how to work out a longitude and latitude by the sun, but never would I qualify as a navigator. *Monsoon's* complement was now navigator, rigger and handyman, local knowledge man and me with the dubious title of "captain".

Pua and Vanaka were nowhere to be found the day before departure and I became quite alarmed. I found my girlfriend, Madeleine, and explained that they had disappeared. In her kind manner, she said there was a difference between me and the Tahitians. I was more or less at home in America because they were my people, but Vanaka and Pua had never been away from their native islands before, never seen highways, or big buildings and did not speak English. They were afraid the authorities would put them in jail on arrival. Madeleine had been to San Francisco so she understood their feelings. Together we went and found Pua and Vanaka drunk as can be. Madeleine explained to them that there was nothing to fear and soon they were looking forward to the experience rather than dreading it.

After spending my last night out in the valley, I bicycled slowly into Papeete, stopped for a cup of coffee, and finally stepped aboard the little schooner. A mixed crowd said farewell: airline employees and stewardesses from Pan Am, friends of Pua's and Vanaka's, and friends from my connection with *Valrosa.* The stern line was let go and the anchor weighed, severing our last contact with the island.

For several days I was afraid to leave the deck, fearing shipwreck, so ingrained was the memory of the *Valrosa.* During the squally conditions Pua and Vanaka proved their worth. With their eyes glued to windward, they sat together on the cabin top; when Vanaka muttered "Mea rahi te mata'i haere mai"—much wind is coming, they would quietly and methodically douse sail, sit stolidly through the rain squall, and just as quietly and methodically set sail again. One evening in a particularly bad squall, when Pua, Vanaka and I were wrestling wet and flogging sails, Hugh, who was fighting at the helm, could be heard whooping above the roar of the storm, "This is my 55th birthday . . . what on earth possessed me to come out here?"

The first of my follies was in stocking the food. I duplicated what we ate aboard *Carronade*: canned corn beef, potatoes, onions, tinned peas and beans and canned fruit, with the addition of two cases of beer, some crackers and cheese. It wasn't surprising that Hugh Gordon couldn't eat the ultra-plain fare, but I really began to worry when Pua and Vanaka, who had previously lived on fish, turned their noses up at Madagascar corned beef every day.

Pua finally found the fishing lines and after catching the first "mahi mahi" took childlike delight in frying up half, and preparing raw marinated fish with the remainder. So after ten days we ate our first good meal. It was warm and sunny and *Monsoon* had been steering herself for the past three days as we gorged ourselves on the best fish in the sea. Hugh ate so much of the raw fish, he made himself sick, lay down for a few hours and on awakening got stuck into it again saying "This is the finest fish I've ever tasted anywhere."

One evening I saw Pua do an amazing trick. He lay down in the scuppers with a flashlight and a gaff hook, lured the mahi mahi with the beam of light, waited for an opportune moment and energetically gaffed the fish straight out of the sea. Only a Polynesian could do it.

There was a language barrier in more ways than one: Hugh refused to accept the fact that I spoke English, saying "I don't know what you speak, boy; I can't understand you." He spoke Portuguese to the Tahitians, but that was a failure, so finally he used slow, concise English and they understood. Pua and Vanaka called Hugh "Monsieur" to his face, and "Le Vieux" when mentioning him to me. The Tahitians have trouble saying "H" so when instructed to call him "Hugh" the best they could do was "oo". I spoke a mixture of French and Tahitian to them, substituting English words I knew they would recognize. They in turn spoke pigeon-French or Tahitian with a few added English words. Pua's first complete English sentence was "Goddamnit, Dass, what the hell you doing?" Their English lessons consisted of gathering round the trans-oceanic radio and listening to American disc jockeys.

My second blunder was not checking *Monsoon* beneath the water, because on starting the engine I found the propeller had no thrust. I took a mask and went over the side and found the prop completely eaten away by electrolysis, which meant we had to sail *Monsoon* right to the dock in Hawaii.

When the island of Hawaii loomed out of the sea, I said to Vanaka and Pua "You see those two peaks, they're almost 14,000 feet high." They both studied the round unimpressive mountains, jabbered between themselves that Tahiti was 8,000 feet and after making numerous comparisons, slowly turned to me saying "Aita, aita"—*sorry, but we don't believe you*. Hugh drew their attention to the blanket of snow covering the peaks. Their jaws dropped—for them snow in Hawaii was a little too much to take. But I must confess, I was equally surprised —snow in Hawaii!

After a gruelling 10 hours to make the last four miles we came to rest in Hilo, Hawaii, from where Hugh flew back to San Francisco. Shortly after stepping ashore he met one of his pilot friends and said "By God, John, am I glad to see you, with two Tahitians and one Australian (he pronounced Australian as orse-tralian) aboard I haven't spoken a word of English for 25 days."

Among the artifacts bequeathed to me by the former owner of *Monsoon* was a small camera, which I gave to Pua for his 45th birthday. Considering he had never owned a camera before and never seen a large supermarket it was not surprising that this scene ensued: like a couple of children they photographed each other wheeling over-laden trolleys of groceries along the alleys, while I pretended to look busy and unembarrassed. Here they were in Hawaii—this was their dream —what stories they would have to tell when they reached home.

We had a pleasant and easy sail up through the Hawaiian chain, Vanaka ticking off the islands as we passed, comparing them with his own Marquesan islands. He told me he owned a great deal of land on his native island of Nuku Hiva. I asked him why he didn't stay there and farm his land. He looked me straight in the eye saying "It is the same reason that you are not at your home farming the land; I like to be able to go and do as I please—the sea is my life." Pua then told me of his land. He was born on the atoll of Hao in the Tuamotus and owned a large portion of a copra plantation until the French decided to seize all their land to build military installations in conjunction with the atomic bomb project on the neighbouring atoll of Muraroa. "They took our land and killed all the fish life!"

Entering the Ala Wai Yacht Harbour, Honolulu, Vanaka was eyeing some bikini-clad girls on the breakwater, Pua was endeavouring to count the forty floors of the Ilikai building (he had never seen more than three floors before), while my eyes were glued to the big black square-rigger with the words CARTHAGINIAN HONOLULU painted across the stern. And to my joy, tied alongside was the *Carronade*. I knew that Andy and Bob and Ken would be mixed up with the square-rigger and, sure enough on berthing the *Monsoon,* Andy said "You're just in time, we're going to sail the big bastard across to San Francisco, leaving in about two weeks time. I think we can get you aboard. Come across and meet the skipper."

TYPE: Baltic-type barque of wood. COUNTRY: U.S.A. OWNER: Tucker Thompson (now owned by the Lahaina Restoration Foundation as a museum ship). YEAR OF CONSTRUCTION: 1921. BUILDERS: J. Ring Anderson, Svendborg, Denmark. DIMENSIONS: Overall length 135 feet; length on deck 105 feet; beam 22 feet 5 inches; draught with 50 tons ballast 9 feet. TONNAGE: 135 tons net. SAIL AREA: 7,000 square feet. RIG: 17 sails, 8 square sails and 9 fore and aft sails. ENGINE: Swedish 6 cylinder Albin diesel, 170 H.P. CREW: 8 on deck.

SQUARE-RIGGER CARTHAGINIAN

On a three-masted barque from Hawaii to San Francisco

Captain Tucker Thompson was a stocky and well-muscled man of about 38. He lived on board with his wife Nita and three children. Tucker used terms like "park the boat", "front" and "back"; but one mustn't be misled by language, as in any profession.

Tucker, behind his casual manner, was no fool when it came to business. He first saw *Carthaginian* (then the three-masted schooner *Wandia*), in Acapulco. As a speculation, he bought her for $15,000 and one week later resold for $64,000 to the Mirisch Film Corporation—who then spent $200,000 converting her into a three-masted barque for the movie *Hawaii*. Tucker remained skipper throughout this period, receiving a handsome salary; on completion of the movie, he bought back the ship for the original $64,000.

When I met Thompson, he explained that everyone making the passage to San Francisco was paying $200. He agreed to take me on and I learnt that Andy, Ken and I were the only non-paying members of the 22 crew aboard. I was to be First Mate and Andy second. (I should explain that my position as Mate over Andy had nothing to do with skill. Tucker hoped I would stay on permanently, whereas Andy would return immediately to *Carronade.*) Thompson proposed to make a shakedown cruise through the Hawaiian Islands in preparation for the passage across to San Francisco. What could be more spectacular than booming under the Golden Gate Bridge in a three-masted barque with all 17 sails set.

I remember my first time aloft: climbing through the maze of rigging, with the ship diminishing in size beneath, up the lower shrouds, over the awkward futtock, up the t'gallant rigging and higher still, swinging out onto the foot-ropes of the royal yard—"laid out" was the old nautical expression. I kept thinking to myself: "I'm fine while the vessel is still fast to the dock, but how about taking in the royal during a gale-wracked night at sea with the masts whipping and the canvas wet and stiff like cardboard, doing its utmost to tear your finger-nails from the very quick."

I had never forgotten a passage written by Alan Villiers of working high up in the masts of a sailing ship: ". . . Once a steel buntline, writhing back over the yard, caught Zimmerman in the head and brought swift blood. He reeled a bit, but carried on. Then after a while we saw that he had fainted, and lay in imminent peril across the yard. For one awful moment the canvas stayed still while we fought to him, and then because we could not take him down we lashed him there. And when we had time to remember him again we found that he had come to, and was working. . . ." Words could not describe the childlike joy I felt with my feet firmly planted on the foot-ropes; leaning over the yard with ribs hooked, grasping the iron jackstay across the top of the yard and both hands dangling free; a good many people would trade their mundane existence with me. I eagerly awaited the day this big hooker would heel to a fresh trade.

Originally two square-riggers were used for the movie, the other being the little hermaphrodite brig *Grethe.* Andy and Bob had already been crew members when she had sailed across to Los Angeles. Bob was not accompanying us on this trip, on the *Carthaginian,* but Andy was and he began filling me in on the procedures of setting sail and handling a square-rigged ship. At night down below we studied books on masting and rigging, then went high into the rigging and discussed various points. The following day with a team each we took a mast and began bending the heavy squaresails as if we had been sailing in square rig all our lives. Right from the start we developed a keen man-to-man competition, Andy with his team on the foremast, I with mine on the mainmast working furiously against one another to see who bent the four sails first. No matter who won, there was always criticism of the opposition's furls or the particular way the robands were made up.

We soon became accustomed to working aloft. We were fit, our hands cal-loused, our general appearance unkempt, our clothes covered with tar, and we reeked of hemp, oakum and marline. *Carthaginian* was no yacht; the work was hard and filthy—tarring rigging, moving pig-iron ballast, and hauling sail. All the while the man-to-man spirit became bitter curse-for-curse competition; even little events like going aloft were always a race. We learnt that the easiest way to come down was by sliding down backstays, and these further developed onto forestays and topmast stays; so a man could virtually go into the rigging and at times work on all three masts without ever touching the deck.

With three ton tackles we set up the 72 deadeyes and lanyards. There were men spread throughout the rigging all trying to outdo the other. Andy swung across to my post at the maintop and began telling me what had happened since we last saw each other in Tahiti: ". . . everything is really working out well for us . . . but the other night we made ourselves a little unpopular with the guy who owns that boat over there," he pointed to a miserable little house-boat on the next pier. "We had a rather noisy party on *Carronade*—a few rums and a few songs—and that guy kept telling us to cut down the noise and we took no notice of him. He finally got so wild he took his pressure-pack fog-horn—and you know how much noise they make—and kept blasting into the night. We kept on; the police came down, arrested him and fined him $50 for disturbing the peace. He's not overjoyed about the whole deal. But seriously though, we've got problems aboard this ship; we've got some good competent guys aboard, and we've got some no-hopers. Like the guy who psycho-analyzes us and reckons the only reason you and I are sailing aboard this hooker is that we want to kill ourselves. "Yeah, he's one, he's got to go—went to the psychiatrist for two years to prove he had a faulty left testicle so he could beat the draft."

As if mirroring our thoughts, Tucker called us to the deck and said: "Boys, we've got too many aboard this ship; the big problem is they've all paid $200 and I can't sack any of them without giving them back their money, but if . . ." and he paused a while, "they were to leave of their own accord, or found the work too hard . . . we don't want men aboard who will let go a line that we might be standing on aloft . . ." Then brushing the matter aside he said: ". . . but I'll leave it up to you boys." When Tucker was gone I stated, "Tucker's a real rascal, but characters like him make the world a better place. Only a guy like Tucker could run a ship like this."

Examples of Tucker's amazing resourcefulness became apparent as the days passed. Various naval officials were given a guided tour of the ship; that evening a truck backed onto the pier and we offloaded several coils of heavy manilla line—compliments of the Navy. In place of Stockholm tar, an essential protective agent aboard square-riggers, Tucker used a tar-based compound used for waterproofing the underside of cars—a very cheap substitute that he had found while looking through Army surplus stores. All of us became closely associated with tarring down rigging and it was soon affectionately known as "Tucker tar". One rainy day while working below decks, we were amazed to find *Carronade's* old rat-lines that had been thrown in the incinerator several months ago. Tucker didn't miss much!

"Can I help?" cried a little voice.

Out on the t'gallant yard with us was Tucker's 10-year-old son, agile and sure-footed as a mountain goat.

"Well, you could help, Toddy, but you can't reach up here."

"Oh, that's all right" he said, "I'm gonna get Dad to put some small foot-ropes on the yards so I can reach."

Ken, who was out on the yard-arm reeving a tackle, called out "Good way to bring up kids, travelling the globe in a square-rigger; good healthy life."

Carthaginian made a three-week shakedown cruise through the Hawaiian Islands to familiarize the crew with setting sail and with manoeuvres under sail, to take on a cargo of large Hawaiian carvings (some 10 feet tall), for sale in California, and to weed out unsuitable crew. It was still dark when we slipped the heavy mooring lines and the black vessel nosed out of Waikiki in the greyness of dawn. She heaved to the ocean swell as all hands turned to sweating down halyards and sheets of the fore and aft sail. As dawn broke several men were sent aloft to cast off gaskets from courses and topsails. Terms foreign to us weeks before broke the early morning air—orders constantly given and rapidly executed—as we "sang out" at the ropes in our hoarsest voices.

With a yacht the halyard is first hoisted, then the sail "sheeted home". The reverse applies to a square-rigged vessel: the gaskets are cast off and the sail then dropped into "its gear". The buntlines, clewlines and leechlines (lines that hold the sail in its gear) are cast off; the sail sheeted home; the halyard hoisted; the yards trimmed to the breeze by a system of braces; and finally someone is sent aloft to "overhaul the buntlines". It took $1\frac{1}{2}$ hours to set sail on our first attempt. One hundred and fifty one lines have to be belayed; it was our duty by the time we finally left for San Francisco to be able to lay our hands on any of these lines on the darkest of nights.

"What about the t'gallants, Tucker?"

"Yeah, let's get it all up".

Tucker hadn't let us bend on the royals or the mizzen topsails, so we put the question to him. "We'll bend 'em going down islands." The spirit was building up. Stan Bettis who had come along as photographer, but who was also a competent sailor, looked aloft at the billowing squaresails and yelled jauntily "A free sheet for Molokai!"

In Molokai we bent the fore and main royals. Jim Kohlor and myself against Andy and Ken; knives glinted as we fastened robands through grommets in the head of the sail, finally seizing it to the jackstay. Two pairs of men, working high up in the sky—"We've got to beat them" grunted Jim. I don't remember who won the race that day, but there were plenty of hard feelings. In Mololai I remember eating so many pineapples that the corners of my mouth began to crack from the acid of the fruit.

On the island of Maui, we took *Carthaginian* into the old whaling port of Lahaina Roads under full sail, gradually shortening sail, and backing the main yards before letting go the anchor—a perfectly executed manoeuvre. Originally Lahaina was the chief whaling port of the Pacific. In 1849, no fewer than 429 whalers anchored in the very same spot where *Carthaginian* came to rest. Whalemen, who had hung their consciences on the Horn, eagerly looked forward to the young wahines who swam out to the whalers to distribute the aloha feeling, and who in return for their hospitality contracted venereal diseases and in-

56

Andy occupied on the Carthaginian in the ancient crafts of a sailor

John Plummer and Des Kearns furling the main course

Mike Myers takes the Carthaginian's wheel

Replacing baggywrinkle from a lofty perch
Gail Chambers takes a bath at sea

Jim Kohler aloft on the main course yard
Heavy weather sailing in true square-rigged style

Landfall on the Californian coast

Tall ship bound for San Francisco

Barque Carthaginian in Ala Wai Yacht Harbour, Hawaii

Andrew Wall and Stan Bettis belay lines after setting sail

Carthaginian spreads all her canvas to the wind

Skipper Tucker Thompson takes a noon sight

Mike Myers, engineer aboard Carthaginia

Ken Mills adjusting a footrope on the t'gallant yard

The original Carronade crew furling the main topsail

Des Kearns lashing a sail

Looking down from the dizzy heights of the royal yard

The new hemp footrope is spliced and served . . .

Then sent aloft . . .

And finally tested

Ken Mills going through the stages of hoisting a sail. On deck Carthaginian had 151 belayed lines

Andrew Wall, working some 90 feet above the deck, takes in the main royal in a heavy squall—using both hands and his teeth

Repairing the spanker gaff at sea

Taking in the flying jib

Andy Wall and Des Kearns share the wheel as the barque ghosts under San Francisco's Golden Gate Bridge

fluenza, which killed off many of the original population. Lahaina is picturesque, but in a forced sort of way. There has obviously been an attempt to retain some of its old charm, but progress and tourism have stifled this.

It was in Lahaina that Tucker, the ever-amazing Tucker, sold *Carthaginian* to the town of Lahaina for $75,000—to be converted into a whaling museum ship as an attraction for tourists. Tucker would remain on as curator and captain, but as he didn't have to surrender the ship till the end of the year, we were still San Francisco bound. A few crew members had already quit on arrival in Hilo, and on departure we accounted for the loss of nine men. Many of them had worked hard and religiously in port but found they couldn't cope working aloft; others found that sailing a square-rigger was anything but romantic—they imagined life at sea as sitting in a deck-chair while the boat sailed itself.

While returning from town Andy and I passed one of the younger crew, a lad of 17 whose father had been before the mast in square-rig and who desperately wanted his son to follow in his footsteps. He had brought his son down and asked Tucker to take him along and make a man out of him; we nicknamed him the "human glow-worm", because he was so devoid of suntan he glowed luminous in the night. Pointing out the seabag on his shoulder, "Where you going, Glowy, laundry?" "No" he replied, almost in tears, "I guess I'm not cut out for this kind of life, I'm going home." and he walked slowly and forlornly down the dock.

"Just goes to show, you can't push a kid into something he's not suited for. I wonder who'll be most disappointed, he or his old man?"—"I know it's sad," said someone at dinner that night, "But what are we going to do, let him come along and have him fall out of the rigging?"

Our crew now stood at eight able-bodied men. "Do you think we can sail with eight?" enquired Tucker. We told him that what we lack in numbers, we make up for in spirit; we could do it all right. There was Tucker; Jim Kohlor, who had previously sailed on Hayden's *Wanderer;* John Plummer, who had just returned from the Vietnam war, parachute division; Stan Bettis, who had recently gone as photographer and narrator with a group who had bought an old ship and sailed to the Galapagos Islands where they planned to set up a Utopia, which Stan described as a "disaster"; Mike Myers, doubling as Engineer, had sailed with the famous Ben Pine when he was alive; Mike Tobin, 16 years old, first trip to sea—but keen to learn, and finally Andy, Ken and myself. In addition to the men there were two girls, Helen, who did the cooking; and the effervescent Gail, who later became a good hand aloft, and equalled any of us at the helm.

It is very seldom in one's lifetime such an opportunity arises: to sail a three-masted barque with new rigging and new sails and a crew such as ours, who water at the mouth at the thought of crowding on canvas and driving her hard till we fetch the Golden Gate.

•   •   •   •

"Psst! Des, wake up . . . I want to show you something on deck." Feeling groggy I looked at my watch. I had only been asleep half an hour. "What the hell do you want?" On trying to get our of my bunk I was thrown violently against the hull. "Jesus," I cried, "What are you doing up there?" "Come on up and see, before Tucker wakes up and spoils it all." The noise of wind and sea was deadened by *Carthaginian's* heavy oak timbers, so I was doubly taken aback as I emerged on deck to find it was blowing wildly and *Carthaginian,* channels down and with an over-powering press of canvas, tore into the night like a thing possessed. I followed Andy to the stern where Ken, giving the helm a careful spoke or two, boasted "Welcome to the watch of real seamen." Mike was sweating, a strange looking tackle leading back to the taffrail. Andy then explained what he had done. Realizing the mizzen topmast was a weak spar, after setting both royals, he had taken the brace leads via the mizzen and back to the taffrail, thus jury-staying the rig and at the same time supporting the mizzen topmast sufficiently to set the mizzen topsail—saying a quick prayer that all three masts didn't come down round his ears. It was highly unorthodox and foolhardy, but it worked. That is until Tucker awoke and ordered the royals to come off.

At the change of watch we learned they logged 38 miles in the four hours—it was our job to better it. As Ken went below he sneered in a voice audible to us all, "They wouldn't have the guts to put the royals back on." Jim and I were on our way to loose the gaskets when Tucker called me back. I thought he was going to say no and I was mentally preparing a protest speech, when he whispered, "the royals . . . and the flying jib" As I weaved up through the rigging I could see Jim keeping even pace on the bucking spars. We "layed out" on the royal yard and cast off gaskets, while from the deck the sail sheeted home and the yard raised and the big black wagon surged half a knot faster. Jim began to whoop with joy. I soon caught the fever and together we gave back yell for yell to the howling southeaster.

One would imagine it difficult to hang on while out on a yard, but it is not. All the weight and strain is taken by the legs, which are firmly planted on the foot-rope, with ribs hooked over the jackstay—not only is it quite comfortable, but it leaves both hands free to tackle the work at hand. Though I must admit at times the old adage of "one hand for the ship and one for yourself" became two hands for ourselves when the only thing we could do was hang on. Below us the others were setting the flying jib. It was sheer lunacy but we tore on—washports clanging.

•　　　•　　　•　　　•

So fired with enthusiasm were we and so whole-heartedly did we throw ourselves into our working of the ship that we did not realize the time passing, and upon raising the Golden Gate none of us were quite prepared for it.

Exactly 130 years ago, a young man named Richard Henry Dana, sailing before the mast in the Brig *Pilgrim,* approached the same San Francisco Bay. He would have been about our age—in his early twenties. He had been an undergraduate of Harvard University, but a weakness of the eyes forced him to give up his studies and undertake the two-year voyage, to cure his eyesight by a complete change of environment, a long absence from books, plenty of hard work, plain food and open air.

At this time, California was Spanish. He described the bay as lying in latitude 37° 58', magnificent, containing several good harbours and surrounded by fertile and finely-wooded country. There was an old fort, the Mission of Delores and near the bight of Yerba Buena trading vessels anchored. There was no other habitation on that side of the bay except a shanty of rough boards put up by a man named Richardson, who did a little trading with the vessels and the Indians. Apparently the next year Richardson built himself a one-storey adobe house on the same spot, long afterwards known as the oldest house in the great city of San Francisco. Dana predicted that if California ever became prosperous the bay would be a place of great importance. At that time he did not realise the magnitude of his prediction.

Carthaginian seemed incongruous with the distant glittering city, the spanning causeway, and the States-line merchant ship standing out to sea. Silhouetted against the setting sun and inspired by the ever-freshening breeze and the bay opening up before us, we squared the yards and let her take a bone in her teeth and move down the channel. Showmanship? Yes but rather than round up to anchor, the opportunity to show off was too much to resist—for many of us it was our last fling in square rig. In the lee of the Island of the Angeles, which Dana called Wood Island, because there he collected firewood, we clewed up and furled all sail "like two pencils one upon the other"—a standard that we hoped would do our forefathers proud.

Upon nightfall we dropped anchor in Sausalito under a high and beautiful sloping hill. Dana spoke of such a hill "upon which herds of hundreds and hundreds of red deer, and the stag, with his high branching antlers, were bounding about, looking at us for a moment, and then starting off, affrighted at the noises which we made for the purpose of seeing the variety of their beautiful attitudes and motions . . ." I am sure it was the same hill.

TYPE: Ocean racing ketch. COUNTRY: U.S.A. OWNER: S. A. Long. DESIGNER: W. H. Tripp & Co. BUILDER: Abeking & Rassmussen. DIMENSIONS: Overall length 73 feet; water-line length 65 feet; beam 16 feet 5 inches; draught 11 feet. DISPLACEMENT: 118,000 lb.; ballast ratio 45%. SAILS: Hard, Hood, & Ratsey. SAIL AREA: 2,670 square feet. RIG: Main, mizzen, jib, genoa, spinnaker. HEIGHT OF MAINMAST: 99 feet. HEIGHT OF MIZZENMAST: 41 feet 5 inches. ENGINES: C.M. 471 (165 H.P.) diesel. ELECTRICAL SYSTEM: 15 kw Onan diesel generator. SPARS AND HULL MATERIAL: Welded aluminium. ACCOMMODATION: 18 people. SPECIAL EQUIPMENT: 2 Smith & Grayson coffee grinder winches; 24 Barrient winches; 3 air-conditioning units; 1 desalination unit; 1 sauna bath; 2 rudders; sound-proof cabins; all-electric galley including a deep freeze. NAVIGATION EQUIPMENT: OMNI, Radio Direction Finder, LORAN A & C, depth sounder, marine sextant.

RACING THE ONDINE

73-foot ketch dismasted on a passage from Greece to Sydney, round the Cape of Good Hope—then first over the line in the 1968 Sydney-Hobart Yacht Race

As the big trans-continental jet lifted off from the shores of America, I thought of the Mediterranean island of Corsica where Sumner A. ("Huey") Long's giant new 73-foot ocean-racing ketch *Ondine* lay moored stern to quay. She was scheduled to make an almost non-stop passage to Sydney, via the Cape of Good Hope to take part in the 1968/69 Sydney-Hobart Yacht Race. But to me this trip meant much more, for it was the final stage of my six-year circumnavigation —and for the first time I would be returning home.

The rock of Gibraltar looked cold in the morning light on 2nd October, 1968. On the slopes the monkeys were preparing for a day of picking tourists' pockets, while round the corner, salty seamen with sheath knives on their belts repaired old gaffers and dreamt of their first sea voyages. The crackle and burble of *Ondine's* Detroit diesel rose to roar like a high-performance racing car. All was in readiness with the crew assembled on deck awaiting the ship's master, Finnish Sven Joffs. Sven raised his hand and the machine swung seaward and south down the coast of Morocco towards the Cape Verde Islands.

On 6th October, we passed within five miles of Grand Canary Island. "Sven, look at all those lights. There's cold beer and women over there. We could be in within the hour, and get some stores too." Back came the reply "If you think the owner's stops were short, you haven't seen mine!"

It was two weeks before *Ondine* struck her first rain squall, laying her ear to the water to listen to the singing bubbles streaking by and the thrash of the deep sea rain. Suddenly from below burst Hank, Nick, Hans and Mitch, nude, with a bar of soap in one hand and a face cloth in the other, and began soaping themselves down. The squall stopped as abruptly as it began, and they were all nicely soaped with nothing to wash it off. There was a rush to catch the small trickles of water from the ends of the booms. Hank, not to be outdone gave the forestay sail a good shaking to get the benefit of the last raindrops. Big Nick, dressed in nothing but a yellow sou'wester hat, yelled towards the sky "God hates sailors". All this time Sven kept his gaze to windward occasionally running his hand through his hair: "Well, that was the first squall and here comes the next."

We could smell the tropics in the air, and it was fascinating to watch the on-coming wall of black cloud and rain, whipped up by approaching white caps. It hit and *Ondine* no longer dipped and rose, but surged ahead in a smother of foam like a sled across a snowfield. Sven took the helm holding it like that of a big windjammer. He turned his pipe upside down to shield the burning dottle from the rain, and with it gripped between his teeth, maintained a determined toothy grimace to windward. "Get the jib off" he said in a quiet voice. As I let go the halyard, Nick, Hank, Dave and Mitch handed in the sail. The water and rain temperature were about 83 °F. and there was great merriment up forward. It was quite a sight—naked, shaven-headed sailors, hauling in sail—Mitch with his half-grown beard and long moustache, looking like one of Pancho Vila's bandidos, Dave buried beneath wet sail and water, and 245-pound Nick, wearing only a yellow sou'wester.

With sail secure, all hands rushed for the booms to catch the remaining water to finish their first freshwater bath (which had taken over an hour) since leaving Gibraltar. Order was restored, the decks steamed in the tropical air, we forgot the squall and wondered what would come next.

We had an official cook on board, the Englishman named Mitch. Sven believed that the content of food was unimportant, as long as it "filled the belly". When Mitch first arrived he made the mistake of asking Sven how he liked his steak. The reply snapped back, "Any goddamn way!" As long as he had his boiled potatoes, Sven was satisfied. It amazed me just how little notice Mitch took of Sven's orders, for he cooked virtually as he wished. On occasions (such as the time Mitch was asked to go to the bakery and get a recipe for baking bread, and the resulting recipe read: "Mix 180 lbs. of flour . . .") Sven would throw his arms in the air with exasperation, storm up forward, and refill his pipe mumbling under his breath "That goddamn cook".

One day Mitch read us a few extracts from his personal log: "We are now 21 days out . . . the crew don't seem to be showing any signs of strain . . ." We thought small wonder!—with 12 hours sleep a day, only two calls to the foredeck to change sails, 24 winches on deck (including two grinders), turkey from our all-electric oven, a sauna bath, three air-conditioning units, hot running water, a de-salination unit and a sound-proofed cabin each.

At meal-times aboard *Ondine*, everyone talked and nobody listened. Seated round a large gimballed table we would dip into the plain, unimaginative food. The cook had given himself the title of "Racing Spoon" and with his shaven head and grimy horizontally-striped T-shirt, he looked like a mid-channel buoy. He sometimes had the temerity to boast that an entire meal had only taken him ten minutes to prepare.

There were two sides to lunch, Sven's and ours. It so happened that we had a surplus of Bulgarian jam and sausage meat known as "Fat Jack's salami", which had remained since the Mediterranean, and we had grown thoroughly sick of both. So, each day it was the accepted chore of whoever was doing galley duty to throw overboard a quantity of both salami and jam without Sven catching him. One had to judge the amount carefully for Sven prided himself on being able to estimate the stores pretty accurately. He never wasted anything—I remember him saving the old ice out of the icebox, which we were cleaning and melting it to scrub the cabin sole.

Sven also had his own tea mug. We would all wash it separately and put it away in its special place with extra care. It was a jade-coloured cast china mug, about 8 inches high. On one side in bold relief were engraved the words "Captain Sven", while on the other was a fully-rigged ship, with the words "Sea Venture Bermuda 1609" and the Latin, *Quo Fata Ferunt* (take fate as it comes). In Argentina the man's drink is gin, and the gauchos of the pampas measure their gin by fingers—a drink is so many fingers high. Similarly, Sven drinks his tea in fingers with a spoon of sugar for each finger. His tea mug, like his pipe was part of his character.

But life on board *Ondine* had another side . . .

Awoken from a deep sleep. Dreams cut short. A light somewhere in the passage-way and your name called: "Roll out, your watch." The Rolex glows in the dark. Eleven-forty. Eyes closed, foul of breath, limbs out of co-ordination; lurch and stumble towards the galley. Boiling water hissing in the pot. Goddamn pot leaks; wish we would get a new one; new pots hard to come by out here. Three men in the galley: Hank, Dave and myself. No one speaks. Half a teaspoon freeze-dried coffee. Easy does it. We've a long way to go—rations—must think of the others. "Survival of the fattest" has no meaning out here. Pour the scalding water. Eyes transfixed into the rich whirling blackness . . . "Why don't I give up this miserable life? What price now; leather chairs and wood fires, fishing rods and trout streams, pine forests and earth-mould scents.

One sugar and stir. Lurch into the darkened saloon and resume customary seat. Curse the angle of heel. Who ever heard of beating into the eye of the trades? Trades are for rolling downwind, warm and gentle. Eyes still half closed with head slumped forward; still no one speaks. Drain the dregs and wash with salt water: to hell with drying, shake the mug and replace it in the rack.

62

Eight bells. Midnight. Stumble on deck. Black, black night. Wind and rushing water and a flying fish flapping in the scuppers. Drowsiness suddenly disappears. Seamen's instincts suddenly come to light . . . a missed footing or hand-hold could mean going overboard. Six luminous dials and the red glow of the compass. The sheets are cracked and the ship flies into the night. Hands grip the wheel. You gauge the heft of the wind and the run of the ship . . .

Hmm! This is the life, maybe I will stay at sea a little longer.

●   ●   ●   ●

The wind has a fetch that goes round the world in the southern Indian Ocean, unchecked by any land. On the night of 16th November, in those latitudes a rising northeaster was making its banshee moan in the rigging as we drive eastward at nine knots, midway on our 13,000 mile delivery voyage from Gibraltar to Sydney. We were racing against time and still on schedule—to reach port early enough to enter Huey Long's new 73-foot ketch in the Sydney-Hobart Yacht Race starting on 26th December.

Cape Town lay 1,500 miles astern; Sydney 5,000 miles ahead. The night was bitter under the wheeling Southern Cross, and the spray that occasionally stung the watch on deck, smacked off those iceberg-freighted seas that stretch away into the blackness to the South Pole.

Our Tripp-designed aluminium ketch fresh from the 1968 Bermuda and Trans-Atlantic races and a summer frolic in the Mediterranean was rolling along with a power we had come to expect.

Huey Long's longtime skipper, Sven Joffs, and seven of us in the crew had been at sea since 2nd October, with just two stops—one of 18 hours in the Cape Verde Islands, off the western bulge of Africa, and one mad 1-hour layover in Cape Town, to take on stores and water. No one wants to sail for ever, no matter how strong the call of the sea; but there comes a time on most extended voyages when you feel you might do exactly that. We were nearing it: our trip so far had been a good one.

Such feelings, however, were shorn in an instant on this night, when, shockingly and cleanly, in a puncture of power and a sound like a city toppling, our 99-foot mainmast cracked and went over the side.

We had been close reaching under double heads'il rig, storm trisail and mizzen. And as near as we can remember, the instant of dismasting occurred when the windward (port, in this case) running backstay and lower spreader failed—but not necessarily in that order. The spar under its great stress of sail and the intermittently smashing sea motion, buckled under the resultant compression strain and broke off four feet below the lower spreaders, leaving a 28-foot stump.

There was no need for the cry of "all hands"—for those below tumbled topside as if they had the galley stove in their pants. We gaped fleetingly at the void against the sky and stars, where our towering mast had once stood, and began coping with the tangled mess of rigging on deck as *Ondine* wallowed in the beam seas.

While we tried to organize ourselves, a number of conflicting thoughts rang simultaneously in my mind: "It is impossible—not the supersonic *Ondine* dismasted? Is there enough mast for a jury rig?" And then the bleak thought "Why not give up this life? You've already been rolled in a gale off Cape Horn and wrecked on a coral atoll in the Pacific."

This was no Sunday sail either: we were wallowing just below the latitude 40 degrees south, along the extreme limit of icebergs, thousands of miles from shore in any direction.

Sven took command of the situation immediately; he seemed to be everywhere at once. Sven has the co-ordination and muscles of a catamount, and skills of command and seamanship that have made him almost legendary, even in the world of global yacht voyaging. He had seen this new *Ondine* through a Europe-South America delivery the previous year, and subsequent Buenos Aires-Rio, Bermuda and trans-Atlantic races. *Ondine* was rolling clumsily in the troughs, and there was some danger of the spreaders puncturing the hull. After we tried unsuccessfully to salvage the broken spar and fittings, Sven decided to cut it away. Had there been the slightest chance of saving it he would have done so.

Oilskins glistened in the glare of flashlights; the lot of us worked on deck for a lurid hour or so, clearing away the rigging and cursing the chilly rain. The decks looked strange round the mast; not a single line or block remained, just the unholy-looking stump.

After we'd salvaged what we could, we lowered the mast into the water, cut the internal halyards, and let it sink into the depths. By the flashlight glare that shone into the icy green waters, we saw hovering beneath the surface, like some spectral sea creature, the remnants of the jib topsail.

What did we do then? Nothing for a bit. We went below for soup and coffee, congratulated ourselves on having plenty of food and water aboard, and enough canvas for a new suit of sails. Tomorrow we'd start on a jury rig and proceed towards Albany in Western Australia, about 3,000 miles away. If we didn't reach Sydney in time for the race, Sven suggested that our hollow stump "would make a fine chimney for Santa Claus". We preferred not to consider it.

We dealt with the masthead as directly as possible in creating a jury rig. Around its gaping aluminium hole, we spliced up a series of strops, which were secured to the masthead by two hooks. From these we rigged new gantlines and halyards. Though the stump itself was certainly sturdy and short enough not to need shrouds for our kind of sailing, we did use two running backstays and the wire luff rope of the storm jib as a new forestay.

We were quite proud of our rig. We could carry full sail in a proper gale, and *Ondine* no longer heeled as much. If anything, we were more comfortable; and life aboard progressed as if nothing had happened. Our cook in his all-electric galley turned out steaks, curries and baked dinners; the ever-ready sauna bath dried our clothes to a warm crispness for the following watch; the three air-conditioning units kept the boat dry and pleasant down below; and we each had projects such as leather work, to keep us well occupied—eight of us in a vessel normally crewed by 21, with all the comforts of home. The only discomforting

64

Ondine prepared for any sail emergency

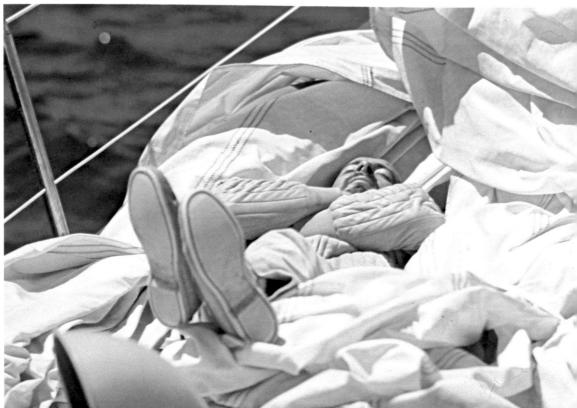

David Parkinson controls the power of the half-million dollar racer
Nick Hylton doing his washing after a tropical rain squall

Clearing the decks after the dismasting
Respite from sail changing in the Hobart race

Ondine blasting to windward under reefed main
Taking sights in the south Atlantic

The fishing fleet, Palermo, Sicily
"Crossing the Line" initiation ceremony

Sven—one of the finest sailors of our time
David Parkinson (U.K.), Hank Wulff (U.S.A.), "Mitch" Mitchell (U.K.), Nick
Hylton (U.S.A.)

First attempts at the jury rig after the dismasting of Ondine

thought was that, shorn of a mast, our arrival and entry in the Hobart Yacht Race, for which we had undertaken this 13,000 mile voyage, now seemed as remote as flying *Ondine* to the moon.

On the eighth day of creditable sailing—after logging 1,000 miles with the jury rig and new suit of sails—we raised Amsterdam Island (midway between Africa and Australia) and, by coincidence, sighted the P & O liner *Canberra* on her route to Durban, South Africa. By radiotelephone Sven spoke to the *Canberra* and sent the following telegram to Huey Long in New York:

ONDINE MAIN DISMASTED NOV. 16. LAT. 41 °S. LONG. 56 °E. UNABLE SALVAGE SPAR. PROCEEDING UNDER JURY RIG TO S.W. AUSTRALIA. SPEED 5 KNOTS.

We presumed with the well-found arrogance of an *Ondine* crew, that Herculean efforts to fabricate and ship a new spar would be made at the other end. And they surely were. Huey Long had owned three *Ondines* over the past 10 years and Sven had been the professional skipper of all three. Their association had been a long one; each respected and depended on the other. Sven was a part of the ship (Long always referred to him as being "married to the boat"), and he only went ashore in half a dozen ports in the world—Panama being one of his favourites. I believe that if Sven definitely thought there was not a chance of making the Hobart Race he would have said so. Therefore he simply stated the facts, knowing that Long would interpret the message and play his part by ordering and flying out a new mast. This was a challenge for Sven, for the eight of us, for Long, for Abeking and Rasmussen (Ondine's builders), for transport companies, riggers—a challenge to unite in readying the *Ondine* for the great race, now exactly one month away. Never in ocean racing history had so much money been spent and so many individuals and organizations united towards a common goal.

Meanwhile, our behaviour offshore mystified the occupants of the French weather station on Amsterdam Island. Because we spoke French, Hans Seyde and I were sent ashore to explain our trouble, and request some diesel fuel—since we still had 2,100 miles to go to our chosen port of Albany. As we pulled away towards the rocky desolate shore, seals surfaced, barking like abandoned dogs round our dinghy. *Ondine* appeared ridiculously out of proportion, having her mast stump half the height of the mizzen—this was the first occasion any of us had been able to see the vessel from a vantage point. Thick patches of kelp, similar to that encountered in Tierra del Fuego a few years earlier, hindered our progress. But we couldn't land safely in the unprotected bay that fronted the remote settlement.

About 30 men had gathered at the end of a crude sea-battered pier to greet us, dancing out of the way as maverick waves broke about their feet. Over the boom of the surf, as we bobbed offshore, we learnt they'd have to request permission from Paris to refuel us, and that would take two to three days, which could be crucial. Since we still had 200 miles of powering ability, which would suffice when close to land, and since our homemade rig was in good order, Sven decided to head south in the Roaring Forties once more.

It took us 16 days to sail from this Indian Ocean outpost to Albany. The weather, though overcast was temperate throughout. By now we'd been at sea for almost three months, and we longed for the land. We figured we must have been at sea too long, because even Sven was talking about what he would do when he got ashore. Hank, Dave and myself calculated we had spent nearly 900 hours on deck together. Have you ever tried to carry on a conversation for 900 hours? Topics become tedious then ridiculous. We knew each other's life histories, had discussed books, films, boats, women, English gentry, the American way of life and Australia. One day when I was looking ahead into the grey loneliness, Dave twisted a quote from the *Wind in the Willows* saying ". . . Fear not, Des m'lad, we will yet gain Australia . . .''

(In 1962, when the old *Ondine* came out to Australia, Huey predicted they would arrive on 26th November at 1400 at Sydney Heads. And 72 days later, at 1406, on 26th November she arrived! It was the most exciting welcome experienced anywhere in the world. There were banners, boats, and tens of thousands of people on Sydney Heads to greet the *Ondine*.) This time we thought we might possibly be sailing in through the heads just as the race boats sailed out on their way to Hobart.

In the Roaring Forties, the days were brightened by our escorts, the great wandering albatrosses. For weeks on end, they wheeled in our wake as we watched, fascinated by their beautiful buffeting manoeuvres in head winds, and their effortless gliding flight along the troughs in search of food. Some stayed faithfully for weeks, and we came to think of them as old friends. "Big Al." was a magnificent specimen with a wingspan exceeding 11 feet, and the smaller "El Stumpo" had the honour of being named after our cropped mainmast. Square-rigger lore says that sailors who die at sea are reborn as albatrosses. If that is so, we must have presented a daunting substitute for the great skysail yarders of yore. However, nowadays in the lonely wastes of the Southern Ocean, perhaps albatrosses live with the philosophy that any company is better than none; and anyway, *Ondine* was a good feeder—some of the square-riggers weren't.

By early December, thoughts of Australia obsessed the ship's company. We were well into the third week since our dismasting; and thanks to Sven's leadership and perseverance, we had averaged 140 miles a day since our last landfall. And always, one topic of conversation was uppermost: could we make Sydney in time to step a new mast before the race. I'll admit, along with most of the others, I didn't think we had much chance. The odds seemed too great.

But the cook, "Our Spoon", didn't think so; when not sleeping, a pastime that seemed to occupy him to the point of fetishism, he was a firebrand of enthusiasm. Midway through our passage from Amsterdam Island to Australia, he produced an official looking sheet on which to chart *Ondine's* daily progress, outside of the navigator's bailiwick. Leaving nothing to chance, he even talked at one stage of sending *Ondine* overland by rail to Sydney, once we'd reached shore. After a while when one crewman too many would ask Sven the length of the previous day's run he'd be told tartly: "Don't ask me, see the cook."

"Racing Spoon" to our amazement and delight, proved the ship's best prophet. His big announcement, made after most of us had given up hope, was that we would arrive in Sydney on December 19th, the same day as our mast would touch down from Germany via the U.S. His prediction seemed impossible; nevertheless, it proved gloriously true—or close enough for *Ondine* to meet her deadline.

· · · · ·

We raised Albany on 10th December. Very few of us had slept the night before in expectation. Under power and sail we approached the rocky coast, with its belts of white beaches. The weather was misty but warm and some of us removed our long underwear. *Ondine* became a beehive of activity, cleaning the boat up ready for port; all hands were in good spirit airing their shore-going clothes and discussing what they were going to do when they got ashore. Dreaming seemed more to the point, for we all knew there would be no holiday if there was a chance of making Sydney on time. We would take on fuel, stores, and water and stand out once more for another 2,000-mile slog to Sydney. If we had joined *Ondine* with the idea of having a vacation or to see the world we were sadly mistaken. To quote Sven again: "If you think Long's stops are short, you haven't experienced Sven's." We had grown accustomed to our short rig and it no longer looked out of the ordinary.

While on the helm, at one stage I was alone on deck and began to consider my position. Looking at the great bulk of Australia I suddenly felt patriotic. For years now I had always been a foreigner in strange countries with strange customs and languages. But now this was my land; I was one of the people; and my shipmates were the foreigners. As I gazed across the grey water at the misty coast, I told myself: no matter what the cost, it has all been worth it—three great capes are now behind . . . Horn, Hope and Leeuwin.

We tied up to a wooden pier near a fleet of whale chasers and were stormed by reporters. It was late afternoon, there were no instructions from Huey, no stores could be taken on until tomorrow, and since Sven owed us a beer from a bet that he lost (he bet us we would not make a 200-mile run in 24 hours under our jury rig) we all adjourned to the Royal George Hotel to drink Sven's beer. We mingled with the crowd; however, I always met the same query "Oh! Yeah, what part of the States are you from?" I was home but no one would believe I was Australian—and I remained a man without a country until all traces of my accent had disappeared. The problem was: I didn't realize I had an accent, the Americans aboard said it was "dinkum Aussie mate" and yet no one ashore would believe me.

Sven surprised us all next morning, dressed in blue yachting jacket, a smartly laundered white shirt, tie, khaki slacks and elk-skin shoes. He looked fifteen years younger. No one had ever seen him look so suave as he sprang ashore to see if there was any news from New York. Meanwhile, our stores arrived, along with the inebriated cook, who explained that each shop he went to insisted on buying him a drink. We took on fuel and lashed extra drums on deck.

About noon Sven burst down the companionway bubbling over with excitement. Apparently Huey, by means of a ham radio had spoken to him personally. The mast would be in Sydney on 23rd December—flown out in three sections that would assemble by a system of sleeves. It would be one-third greater in wall thickness and one inch greater in diameter. Atmosphere rose to a fever pitch as Sven waved his arm in a motion signalling us to cast off and get under way. "How Long did it I don't know," said Sven as we roared down the harbour. Sven still had his tie on, and was even more enthusiastic than we were (this was not the Sven we once knew). "He wanted to know how the gear situation was and whether the boys would still like to stay on for the race." Sven almost choked on his next words, "I told him we would have to prize them off the boat now." Everyone looked at each other and their faces reflected grim determination, comradeship and a common aim to get the boat to Sydney as fast as possible—and by God we would.

The Great Australian Bight lived up to its reputation, turning on the most miserable conditions since Gibraltar. All we could do was laugh at each other's discomfort. A standard joke throughout the 1,000-mile crossing was: "Never mind if we burn out the engine, someone will fly one out by helicopter." Sven kept *Ondine* close inshore going through Bass Strait and virtually "crushed crabs" going up the New South Wales coast to avoid the southerly current. At 11 o'clock at night, we crept through Sydney Heads—a quiet and unimpressive entry. I took the helm down the harbour, though I must confess, I didn't recognize a single landmark. I didn't feel anything—it was just like another port. We tied up at the Cruising Yacht Club of Australia, along with all the other race boats. Yacht *Ondine*: 80 days and 13,000 miles out of Gibraltar . . . It was 21st December, four days before the start and two days before our mainmast was to arrive.

•   •   •   •

Next morning all hands were called and we were busily at work preparing *Ondine* for the race.

How did all the pieces come together? There was a five-week evolution of trans-oceanic creativity and consternation that will doubtless never be equalled in the annals of ocean racing. On receipt of Sven's original wire, Huey, who could only guess at the cause of dismasting, flew immediately to Germany where, with *Ondine's* builders, Abeking and Rasmussen, he decided on a slightly heavier aluminium replacement. The yard, whose first reaction had been incredulity when informed of the building and shipping schedule, finally took on the commission as a challenge. They dropped all other work and completed the new spar within five days.

To facilitate shipment, the mast was made in three sections, the largest being

41 feet. To simplify assembly at the other end the sections were given a sleeve and screw arrangement, which would obviate last minute welding. Meantime the East End Supply Company of New York airfreighted to Australia replacements for rigging and all fittings that had been lost overboard or destroyed during dismasting. Then transport difficulties arose: One quote, on a compartment-occupying basis, for shipping the mast was an astronomic $38,000. Dissent and rounds of discussion followed hard on one another. Eventually, TWA and Qantas co-operated in a salty goodwill gesture and transported the lot to Sydney for $4,000.

The mast was scheduled to leave U.S. on 21st December by Qantas, the same day we arrived in Sydney. Airline authorities in New York removed a bulkhead to accommodate the mast, and delivered it to Sydney Qantas terminal on 23rd December at 6 a.m. Total cost of building and shipping: $40,000. The mast was rushed to the Royal Australian Navy Yard on Garden Island. An American destroyer, whose captain was an old school mate of Huey's, stood by in case we needed anything, as did the entire services of the Australian Navy. For the assembly and stepping, Graham Shields, had closed his mast making factory, and his entire staff of 23 men spent 30 hours working round the clock. At noon on 24th December, *Ondine* had her new 99-foot mast; it was about 330 pounds heavier than the original.

All this time, Huey Long was pacing the floors of several air terminal waiting rooms between San Francisco and Hawaii. Having missed his Qantas plane because of a late connecting flight to San Francisco on 22nd December, he made it to Honolulu via PAN AM. with his 12-year-old son, Russel. Thence with the friendly assistance of Australian pal Sir James Kirby, he found air space to Sydney, joining the boat just a day before the race. At the same time other members of our 21-man crew arrived. Dave Elwell, ex-crew member of the 12-metre *Intrepid;* Don Wakeman, Sparkman and Stephens rigging expert; Ted Turner, owner of the 12-metre *American Eagle,* who boasts, "I tried to get a syndicate together to buy the Eagle but there were no takers, so I bought it myself" and many other veteran ocean racers.

We spent Christmas Day adjusting rigging and getting gear on board. There were three of us up the mast together and I remember looking enviously from my perch at the people sipping cocktails and indulging in Christmas cheer on the patios and verandas of the homes on the hill opposite the yacht club.

At 8 a.m. on 26th December, the morning of the race, we cast off and moved down the harbour looking like a super dreadnought among all the other craft. We boxed the compass and simultaneously tuned the rig, a crucial task that under normal circumstances occupies racing skippers several days. We set our new main only to find it was 18 inches too long on the hoist, and therefore could only be carried efficiently to windward with a Cunningham reef. Fifteen minutes before the start, we set the huge genoa, and in a harbour gone mad with hundreds of spectator boats dogging the 65 race entries (including 16 foreigners), began the countdown manoeuvring, for which *Ondine* had sailed half way round the world.

69

We beat down Sydney Harbour, and in the early pandemonium couldn't even determine our position in the fleet. Just as we passed the Heads, we sighted the powerful sloop *Rage* ahead and two crack Australian boats, *Ragamuffin* and *Koomooloo,* close astern. Round South Head, we set our giant chute. The others followed suit and we all shaped a course southwards down the coast. Within four hours we had the entire fleet hull down astern, and settled down to a false sense of racing and personal comfort.

The Tasman Sea erupted predictably on the very first night, with a plague of thunderstorms, torrential rains and sudden frustrating calms. Aboard *Ondine* we had a night-long Chinese fire drill with countless sail changes, among hoarse shouts of command from cockpit to foredeck, and equally hoarse and lurid rejoiners from the "deck apes" who could never quite change the rags fast enough for Huey. "Now" was his customary demand, but what he meant was "five minutes ago".

With a 21-man crew constantly wet, the sauna bath was the most popular resurrecting convenience aboard. It did have its hidden hazards, however. At the change of one watch, one crew member emerged on deck with an ear-to-ear grin, holding a bit of grotesquely twisted pink plastic. He said, "I wouldn't recommend drying out any more flashlights in the sauna." After dodging many waterspouts, and sending Nick Hylton aloft to re-reave a failed jib topsail halyard, we sailed into a bad bath of light and miserable conditions. Late on the second night, however, the wind returned with a vengence and blew a gale from the southeast with gusts to 50 m.p.h. Under reefed main and foresail, *Ondine* went pile driving through the seas at 9 and 10 knots, even with shortened rig. And we knew that no one in the fleet could stay with us under these conditions. The Australian yacht *Starfire of Perth* had been leading the racers boat for boat. But by 29th December after the strong southerlies had battered the yachts, causing 13 dropouts, and had blown many west of the rhumb line in the Bass Strait, we were out in front again. The Sydney sloop *Ragamuffin* however was giving us trouble right along.

The wind was blowing 35, and we were down to staysail and reefed main, blasting along to windward with cracked sheets at 8 knots. Some of the crew were sick, and I didn't feel too sharp myself. At times we seemed to drop free into the bottom of a trough, only to roar up the face of the next wave and explode through its top. "We won't have to wash the decks down this morning." Off the forbidding Tasman coast that night the wind shifted northeast. We set our huge striped chute again, riding with it towards the mouth of the Derwent River at 10 knots. A saffron dawn lit the pipe organ cliffs of Tasman Island. *Ondine* shortly afterwards went scudding upriver and over the line to finish first, to the accompaniment of frenzied cheering by thousands of people flanking the banks of the Derwent.

"Giant Victor" is what the papers called us, and giant we must have seemed carrying a 4,600-square-foot spinnaker billowing from deck to mast-head. Barely 50 yards from the thunderous finish line came the classic comment of the race. Ted Turner of Atlanta shouted back to Huey at the helm: "Well, Huey, no matter what it cost, it was worth it."

•　　•　　•　　•

My voyage on *Ondine* had a much greater effect on my future life than I had imagined on that long flight from New York to Corsica four months before.

In Gibraltar, after only four days I had proposed to a girl who hitched a ride with us from Athens, and parted from her until our agreed rendezvous in Sydney the following January.

On January 17th, just 12 hours after the indefatigable *Ondine* left on a non-stop passage to Panama, this girl Susie arrived from England.

The day before, realizing I was stone broke, I asked Sven what would become of the old mast stump. He told me that, in theory, it belonged to the insurance company, but if it had been his to give away, he would gladly give it to me. I thought this over for a moment, and on an impulse, telephoned a scrap metal company and sold the stump. The following morning I arrived home, $60 richer, a souvenir 2" section of the mast under one arm and my wife-to-be on the other.

A few weeks later we were married in a tiny timber and corrugated iron church, set amid palm trees on tropical Lord Howe Island, 450 miles off the N.S.W. coast—a fairytale ceremony attended by the islanders who had, within hours of our arrival, decorated the church and organized a reception at Government House for two complete strangers to make it one of the most delightful and unforgettable days in their adventurous life together.

Photographic data

Initially I bought a 20-year-old Nikon, which incorporated the old range-finder focusing system and the standard 55mm 1.4 lens. The camera survived continual exposure to sea water, hot tropical sun and sand.

For the Cape Horn passage Andy Wall provided the Nikonos II, with a 35mm 3.5 lens. This camera proved ideal for rough and wet high-latitude sailing, and was used successfully to photograph a wreck in 90 feet of water in French Polynesia.

Towards the end of my journeys I graduated to the Nikon F Photomic TN and used two bodies with 28mm, 55mm, 105mm and 200mm lenses.

Action photos were the most difficult, for I was always involved with the task at hand, so I designed and built a housing for the Nikon that I call an "Acfoto Unit". It is equipped with shutter release coupling and winding-on mechanism, but I had to forego the Photomic head and metering system and build a through-the-top viewing system. The unit sits on my chest and is held by a harness arrangement. Because of restricted area and the need for speed, I use only the 28mm lens as it has a wide field of vision and easy focusing.

This enables me to handle sails, work aloft or be involved in an emergency and still capture the moment.

Cameras and films on these journeys had a lot of hard use and stood up well. Films used: COLOUR: Kodachrome II; Kodachrome X; Ektachrome; High speed Ektachrome. MONOCHROME: Plus-X and Tri-X (Kodak).

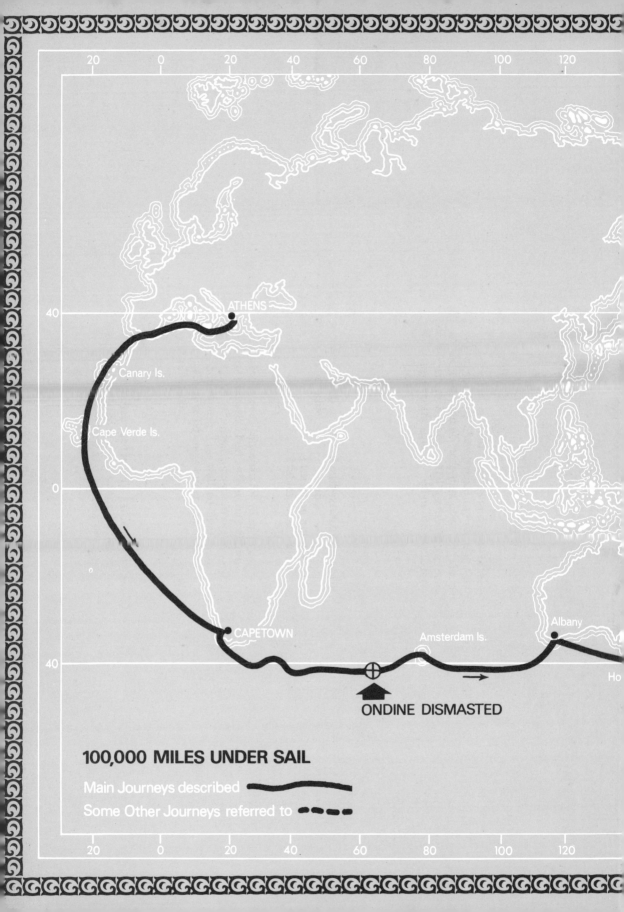

ATHENS

Canary Is.

Cape Verde Is.

CAPETOWN

Amsterdam Is.

Albany

⊕
⬆
ONDINE DISMASTED

Ho

100,000 MILES UNDER SAIL

Main Journeys described ━━━━━

Some Other Journeys referred to ━━ ━━ ━━